Tales of Tongue Fu

by Paul Krassner

Introduction by David Jay Brown

Illustrations by Trina Robbins & Pete Von Sholly

Ronin Publishing
Berkeley, California

Tales of Tongue Fu

Published by
Ronin Publishing, Inc.
PO Box 22900
Oakland, CA 94609
www.roninpub.com

Production:

Editor:	Beverly A. Potter, Ph.D.—docpotter.com
Cover Design:	Brian Groppe—briangroppe.com
Cover Illustration:	Pete Von Sholly—vonshollywood.com
Book Design:	Beverly A. Potter
Illustrations:	Trina Robbins—trinarobbins.com
	Pete Von Sholly

Fonts:
Baskerville—Mscrosoft; Bookman Old Style—Adobe; Chankbats—Chank; Couchlover—Chank; Holstein—Ethan Dunham; Marker Felt—Atech

Library of Congress Card Number: 2007939444
Distributed to the book trade by **PGW/Perseus**
Printed in the United States by **Inner Workings**

An America married couple, who both worked for the Census Bureau, had their baby early—by induced labor—so that it could be included in the decade's statistics This book is for that kid.

—Paul Krassner

When you are joyous, look deep into your heart, and you shall find it is only that which has given you sorrow that is giving you joy. When you are sorrowful, look again in your heart, and you shall see that in truth you are weeping for that which has been your delight.

—Kahlil Gibran

People use *The Prophet* to get laid.

—Lenny Bruce

Paul Krassner is the funniest man in the galaxy and this is his best book.

—Robert Anton Wilson

... a contemporary Kahlil Gibran

—Baba Ram Dass

Books by Paul Krassner

One Hand Jerking:
Reports from an Investigative Satirist

Confessions of a Raving, Unconfined Nut:
Misadventures in the Counter-Culture

Impolite Interviews

How a Satirical Editor Became
a Yippie Conspirator in Ten Easy Years

Magic Mushrooms and Other Highs:
From Toad Slime to Ecstasy

Psychedelic Trips for the Mind

Pot Stories for the Soul

Best of the Realist

The Winner of the Slow Bicycle Race:
The Satirical Writings of Paul Krassner

Sex, Drugs & the Twinkie Murders

Murder at the Conspiracy Convention

Table of Contents

... most of the famous swamis are hip show-
biz operators, campy-vampy-splashy-flashy
homosexual queens with gullible followers,
grand ashrams, triumphal road tours, performing restful magic. It's amusing to hear
them gossip and put each other down. They
follow each other's productions like jealous
rockstars. Competing for the top of the cosmic charts."

–Timothy Leary
The Fugitive Philosopher

Introduction

By David Jay Brown

Imagine all the sensuous fun you could have with a fifteen inch tongue that instantly responds with lightening-speed precision to your every intention. The erotic possibilities alone seem endless, but just think of the deity-like super powers that you would command in every sphere of human activity with such an enchanted, tentacle-like extension of your biological machinery.

The genetically-altered hero of the wonderfully weird and deliciously strange story that you now hold in your hands—Tongue Fu—has this amazing ability, like a preternatural frog and fairy tale prince rolled into one. However, like the enlightened masters of the East who—supposedly—gain extraordinary psychic powers—or *sidhis*—through advanced yogic meditation, Tongue Fu isn't easily distracted by these superhuman abilities, and he stays unwaveringly focused on his uniquely surreal spiritual path throughout his madcap adventures on the fringes of American culture and the frontiers of human consciousness.

Tales of Tongue Fu—Paul Krassner's profoundly funny and hysterically wise satirical novel about

the genetically mutated son of a Japanese kamikaze pilot and an American Army nurse—will have
you rolling on the ceiling with laughter. Krassner is
a world-class master of great satire and one of the
funniest comedians on this wayward planet. He is
well-known as a stand up comic, and many comedians and writers—such as George Carlin, Lenny
Bruce, Matt Groening, and Kurt Vonnegut—have
attributed some of their comedic inspiration to
Krassner—who, incidentally, also turned Groucho
Marx on to LSD. The mind-altering satirical writer
Robert Anton Wilson—author of the *Illuminatus!* tril-
ogy—said "Paul Krassner is the funniest man in the
galaxy and *Tales of Tongue Fu* is his best book."

Laughter Opens the Mind

In *Tales of Tongue Fu* Krassner mischievously pokes
fun at all forms of spirituality—from fundamentalist
preachers to New Age gurus. The hilarious monologues
by Anal Roberts and Baba Blabla are alone worth
the price of this book. But don't let Krassner's deliri-
ously hilarious antics fool you—there is some pretty
serious wisdom in this book. In fact, Ram Dass—the
world renown spiritual teacher and author of *Be Here
Now*—called Krassner "... a contemporary Khalil Gibran." *Tales of Tongue Fu* cleverly and alchemically
blends together sidesplitting humor with some unusually profound philosophical insights into the evolution
of consciousness and the nature of existence.

Like a strange memetic crossbreed between Herman
Hesse's *Siddhartha*, the television show *Kung Fu*, and *Mad
Magazine* on acid, Krassner's zany and profound philosophical insights will have you simultaneously laughing
out loud and staring into the Heavens with wonder.

A Trickster

Probably best known for helping to found the political prankster movement known as the "Yippies" (he coined the term), and for publishing the first adult satire magazine, *The Realist*, Krassner is an unusually gifted, multifaceted trickster. *The Realist* blurred the distinction between actual news and fictitious humor, and it was often very difficult to tell the difference—which was precisely why the magazine was so much fun. Krassner's irreverent and egalitarian mockery of everything and everyone makes him a delight to read, and his unique brand of cultural satire and enlightened comedy appears to be perfectly tailored for the ever-expanding digital cyberculture that is now emerging on this planet.

Krassner draws from the exponentially-growing, planetary-wide—mainstream and underground—cultural mediasphere as a source for his satirical substrate. The mass media reflects the soul of the civilization from which it arises, and this allows Krassner to shamanically utilize insightful references from television shows, popular music, comic books, and other forms of mass media to simultaneously elicit laughter and elevate awareness, transforming seemingly mundane aspects of the world into reflections of the miraculous. Playful word puns, and clever twists on current media trends, are woven with wit into Krassner's wonderfully weird, wild, and whimsical adventure, adding smiles and laughs to his masterfully-expressed revelations.

Krassner's revelations have enormous power and evolutionary potential. Like the Yippie media pranks of the Sixties, Krassner's jokes often conceal hidden layers of deeper meaning, and his insights and ideas have a strong tendency to evoke conversation; i.e., replicate themselves, using our brains to spread them like a virus. This is akin to what media theorist Douglas Rushkoff would call a "media virus," or "a media story that carries a cultural message beyond the actual story." As you read through *Tales of Tongue Fu*, your nervous system will become "infected," so to speak, with Krassner's replicating revelations that will in turn "infect" the brains of those around you, and, ultimately, help to raise consciousness on the planet. Krassner's magical book accomplishes this superior cognitive programming by invoking a trance state and slipping powerful subliminal messages into your subconscious mind as you read through it. In other words, simply reading this book helps to make the world a better place.

When I interviewed Krassner for my book *Conversations on the Edge of the Apocalypse*, he offered some insight into this process by pointing out how humor can be used as a vehicle for educating people, i.e., reprogramming their brains. He told me that "when you make an audience laugh their defenses are down. It's no matter that they come from disparate backgrounds. At that moment that they're all laughing at what you said, they're united—and they're united in accepting a truth that the humor points out. At its best, humor is a vehicle for truth. People don't like to be lectured at. When they laugh, and their defenses are down, this means that they have less resistance to a truth then they may have had before."

Be Forewarned

Ready or not, Krassner has "ways of making you laugh," and laughter is Krassner's means of elevating consciousness and expanding awareness— which now appears to be necessary for our survival on this planet. According to world renown chaos theorist Ervin Laszlo, our species is on a highly self-destructive path, and—due to global climate change, pollution, and a multitude of nonsustainable human activities—we only have a few years left to turn things around before we irreversibly damage our biosphere and end civilization as we know it. We appear to be living in a time where each and every decision that we make carries great importance in determining our future and only by raising global consciousness can we survive.

Electronic, cross-cultural interconnection appears to be key to our survival. The integration of Asian and American cultures is an important theme in *Tales of Tongue Fu,* and this intercultural fusion reflects the cross-cultural fertilization that is currently occurring between the Far East and the Wild West, reflecting a hopeful, planetary-wide, boundary-dissolving trend.

If our consciousness and technology continue to evolve together, hand-in-hand—and we don't destroy ourselves and our precious biosphere—we can all look forward to the soon-to-arrive day when nanotechnology, advanced robotics, and artificial intelligence will allow us to live in a virtually utopian, transhuman world of great abundance, free of aging, disease, and poverty, where everyone will have the ability to genetically morph their body according to the will of their imagination. When humanity's golden era of technological and spiritual achievement arrives, every man, woman, and child will be able to stand tall, look boldly into the horizon, and proudly sport a fifteen inch tongue that instantly responds with lightening-speed precision to his or her every intention.

—David Jay Brown

Preface

by Paul Krassner

In 1971, after reading Ed Sanders' book about the Charles Manson mini-cult massacre, *The Family*, I began my own investigation to see if I could find any answers to the questions he raised. The complete story, "The Rise of Sirhan Sirhan in Scientology," is the longest article in my collection, *One Hand Jerking: Reports From an Investigative Satirist*, but in this context, I'll just quote an excerpt from my interview with Preston Guillory, a former deputy sheriff in Malibu who participated in the raid on the Spahn Ranch where Manson and his cohorts were arrested. Conspiracy researcher Mae Brussell put me in touch with him.

"A few weeks prior to the Spahn Ranch raid," he told me, "we were told that we weren't to arrest Manson or any of his followers. We had a sheaf of memos on Manson—that they had automatic weapons at the ranch, that citizens had complained about hearing machine guns at night, that firemen from the local fire station had been accosted by armed members of Manson's band and told to get out of the area. Deputies started asking, 'Why aren't we gonna make the raid sooner?' I mean, Manson's a parole violater,

we know there's narcotics and booze. He's living at
the ranch with a bunch of minor girls in complete
violation of his parole. Deputies at the station quite
frankly became very annoyed that no action was being taken about Manson."

"What did you guys speculate the motivation behind that protection was?" I asked.

"My contention is this—the reason Manson
was left on the street was because our department
thought that he was going to launch an attack on
the Black Panthers. We were getting intelligence
briefings that Manson was anti-black and he had
supposedly killed a Black Panther. Manson was a
very ready tool, apparently, because he did have
some racial hatred and he wanted to vent it. But
they hadn't anticipated him attacking someone
other than the Panthers. You have to remember
that Charlie was on federal parole all this time from
1967 to 1969. Do you realize all the shit he was getting away with while he was on parole? Now here's
the kicker. Before the Tate killings, he had been
arrested at Malibu twice for statutory rape. Never
got [imprisoned for parole violation]. Manson liked
to ball young girls, so he just did his thing and he
was released, and they didn't put any parole hold
on him. But somebody very high up was controlling
everything that was going on and was seeing to it
that we didn't bust Manson."

So, did racism in the Sheriff's Department make
them collaborators in a mass murder? I found myself gathering scary pieces of a mind-boggling jigsaw
puzzle, without any model to pattern it after. Ultimately, in 1972, I experienced a bizarre freakout
from information—and misinformation—overload.
Then, in 1973, I wrote this New Age media fable,
Tales of Tongue Fu—which served as a catharsis

for me—and in 1974 it was serialized in Stewart Brand's *Co-Evolution Quarterly*. I began only with the name of my protagonist, Tongue Fu—a man with a 15-inch tongue—as a takeoff on *Kung Fu*, a popular TV series at the time.

During the late 1960s and early 1970s, the Vietnam war was peaking, while back in America the counterculture was peaking on psychedelics. Sex, drugs and rock'n'roll was a slogan, but at the core of it there was a spiritual revolution, with young people abandoning western religions of control and experimenting with eastern disciplines of liberation. One of the threads in this book parodies the plethora of those who attempted to enhance and/or exploit that search for expanded consciousness.

Charlie Manson acted as a perverted version of such gurus. Indeed, a member of his family, Squeaky Fromme, who later attempted to assassinate then-President Gerald Ford, was the basis of the frizzie-haired hippie character in *Tales of Tongue Fu*. This all took place before personal computers—I depend on mine), the Internet—I practically worship it, cell phones—I've adapted to one), the remote—I never touch my TV set any more, Web sites—I have one, YouTube—I'm on it, Tivo—I have no need for it, and having to take your shoes off before you can get on a flight—kids growing up these days will think it was always that way.

A Period Piece

Beverly Potter, my publisher at Ronin, suggested updating references—Alice Cooper could become Marilyn Manson, *Dating Game* could become *Love Connection* and underground publications could become zines, which have already become outdated by blogs—I do 'em—to bring the time frame forward because many readers weren't born yet, but I felt that for the very same reason the book should remain as a "period piece," so that the climate then can be compared and contrasted with the climate now. For example, the members of Better Your Exit (BYE) in *Tales of Tongue Fu* are forerunners of the suicide bombers coming out of the Middle East.

I originally got the idea for BYE from an interview I did with Woody Allen in 1965:

Paul: "Are you concerned about the population explosion?"

Woody: "No, I'm not. I mean, I recognize it as a problem which those who like that area can fool around with. I doubt if there's anything I can do about the population explosion, or about the atom bomb, besides vote when the time comes, and I contribute money to those organizations who spend their days in active pursuit of ends that I'm in agreement with. But that's all. And I'm not going to set fire to myself."

Paul: "But do you agree with the motivations of the Buddhist monks who set fire to themselves in Vietnam?"

Woody: "I don't think so. No, I think that they don't know what they're doing. I think they're nuts. That's *not* the answer. When all is said and done, it's not the answer. When you're home at night, and you say to yourself, 'Tomorrow morning I'll get up at eight o'clock and set fire to myself,' there's something wrong. I wouldn't do it that way. I can see dying for a principle, but not *that* way. At the very minimum, if you are going to die for something, you should at least take *one of them* with you. Go back to the Jews in Germany. If you have a loaded gun in your home, and the state comes to get you, you can at least get two or three of *them*. I'm not opposed to violence as a course of action in many instances. Sometimes passive resistance is fine, but violence in its place is a good and necessary thing. But setting fire to yourself is not the answer. With my luck, I would be un-inflammable."

Consider, then, this confession in *Tales of Tongue Fu*:

"Recently I went and got programmed for forty days at Aripoff Center in Chile where there were some U.S. Army colonels hanging around. Then I went and got deprogrammed for forty nights at Exedrin Institute in Big Sur where I recognized those same colonels hanging around, only now they were generals. Well, one night I was soaking in the hot spring sulphur baths and I overheard them discussing a scenario that gave me the chills. They were talking about a squad of their personnel from Special Forces who plan to claim that they're revolutionary BYE terrorists and hold our whole government hostage with just a few home-made nuclear devices...."

One person's paranoia is another person's satirical prophecy.

Enjoy your ass off.

—Paul Krassner

Part One

1

Captain Mediafreak Takes a Trip

Click!

The Statue of Liberty is wearing a huge bra. A disembodied female voice asks in a sultry whisper: "Do *your* huddled masses yearn to breathe free?"

Click!

A young man in Army fatigues is juggling several teargas grenades and rifles-with-bayonets-extended alternately in the air, accompanied by the band playing a schmaltzy rendition of *Come On, Baby, Light My Fire.*

Click!

"—confessed to police today," a newscaster is saying as he taps his foot in rhythm with his speech, "that he had been hired by a Safeway Supermarket to put *Kosher for Passover* labels on canned foods which were not actually kosher—"

Click!

Striding barefoot in the sunset along 42nd Street comes Tongue Fu. Under a floppy hat and bangs-covered forehead, his eyes reveal an ancestry that is half Japanese and half American. He is carrying a rolled-up sleeping bag. On his back is a knapsack.

It has been a lengthy journey. First, a freighter across the Pacific Ocean. Then, a bus from San Francisco to New York City. Now he stands on the sidewalk, watching with fascination as a pizza maker throws his lump of dough over and over toward the ceiling.

After a little while, the pizza maker scowls at him through the large window that separates them. In response, Tongue Fu parts his lips slightly. Gradually, he sticks out his tongue at the pizza maker, inch by mottled red inch.

The pizza maker ogles in amazement. For Tongue Fu's tongue is approximately fifteen inches long. The lump of dough falls on the pizza maker's head while he stares in disbelief.

Tongue Fu walks away, a satisfied expression on his face....

FLASHI€BACKI€:

The venerable teacher, Say When Daddy, glazed blind eyes set off by a white Van Dyke goatee, holds out a small item in his hand.

"Anteater," he says to young Tongue Fu—placing him at a proper distance by putting his other hand on the freshly-shaved head of his student and biological son—"quickly, snatch this peyote button from my hand."

Out darts Anteater's unusually long tongue. But Say When Daddy closes his fist with plenty of relative time to spare. He smiles with patient understanding.

"Tough nookie," he says. "You must always remember that whether your gift of tongue is to be a curse or a blessing depends upon how skillfully you learn to manipulate it. Only after you have thoroughly mastered the art of liberation will you be able to flow with the commerce of exploitation which is the other side of that coin along whose ridged edge you wish to roll through life. All right, Anteater, you may put your tongue back in your mouth now...."

Inside an abandoned Times Square newsstand, Captain Mediafreak is tripping in his basket. He has no legs and only one arm. At the exact instant that a temporary power failure shuts off his color television set, Tongue Fu knocks on his door.

Captain Mediafreak gets an adrenalin rush as his heartbeat suddenly increases. He hardly ever has visitors. He points his TV channel selector, trigger finger ready, at the tall stranger who begins to enter and speaks in a halting manner.

"Please. I do not intend to startle you. I merely seek shelter for the night."

"Hey, that's really weird. I was just watching you on the tube. I must've dropped too much acid this time. Every Thursday evening I ingest a few tabs of LSD as my own private religious ritual."

"Is not too much enough?"

Captain Mediafreak nods his curly blond head, upon which sits an American Airlines Junior Astrojet pilot cap.

"Anyway," he says, "of course you can stay here." He lights a candle. "I sure hope the power goes back on soon. Norman Mailer's on Dick Cavett tonight."

Tongue Fu empties out his knapsack, which, except for a custom-tailored edition of the *I Ching,* a cooking pot, a box of matches, packets of herbs, a toothbrush and a kazoo, is completely filled with soybeans.

"Listen," Captain Mediafreak says, "how come you did that thing to the pizza maker with your tongue?"

"I am a mutation. That is all I know."

"No, I don't mean *how.* I mean *why?*"

"It was an act of altruism. The pizza maker now has a new daydream to occupy his mind when he is working. Also a conversational tidbit to share with his friends."

Tongue Fu rolls out his sleeping bag onto the floor. He sits on top of it in the lotus position. His hands hover just above his knees, palms upward, thumbs and forefingers forming a bridge by curving his outstretched tongue around at a right angle.

"Wow," says Captain Mediafreak, "I'll bet you can give yourself great head."

Tongue Fu withdraws his tongue back into his mouth in order to answer.

"I do not. I remain celibate so long as I continue in search of my soulmate. But first I must find my mother. And my sister. I have never known either. That is why I have come to America."

When the electricity returns, Dick Cavett is asking: "Do you write better before or after sexual intercourse?"

"During," replies Norman Mailer, switching to W.C. Fields' voice. "One might even say that one best lubricates one's heroic writing instrument with the tart nectar of Bartholin's glands."

2

Tongue Fu
Meets His Mother

In a funky mid-Manhattan apartment, a
dignified grey-haired woman in a nurse's uniform is dust-
ing her Tiffany kerosene lamp. She is waiting for a visit
from her son. She hasn't seen him since he was an infant.

Outside, the pace on this Friday afternoon is
restless. Tongue Fu observes people rushing along
the sidewalk only to stand on line for a bus. A traffic light signals *Don't Walk,* and he is bypassed by
citizens hurrying frantically across the street.

"When the sign says *Do Not Walk,*" Tongue Fu
remarks to a hot chestnuts vendor on the corner, "it
is perceived as *Run.*"

"It don't say Do *Not,* it says *Don't,* can'tcha read
English, buddy?"

"Yes. But I do not ever use contractions."

"Oh yeah? Why don'tcha?"

The traffic light signals *Walk.* Tongue Fu smiles
at the hot chestnuts vendor and shrugs his shoulders as he steps off the curb. When he reaches the
other side of the street, he sees a metal tab in the
gutter, discarded from the top of a soda pop can. He
automatically picks it up .

FLASHIEBACKIE:

Walking along the beach, Say When Daddy steps on a jagged piece of glass, broken off from a Coca-Cola bottle. Wincing, he draws young Tongue Fu's attention to it.

"Did you not take notice of this object," the blind old man asks, "that which now causes my foot to bleed so profusely onto the sand?"

"I am sorry, Master."

"No, do not apologize. But you cannot attain true inner peace without practicing responsibility. You must walk along this beach each morning and pick up whatever might prove dangerous to someone else."

"How long must I continue to practice such responsibility?"

"Until you find yourself doing so without being aware any longer of the reason."

"But suppose I am the only one to do this?"

"Why, then, Anteater, you should be pleased, for that will show you have no ulterior motive, such as wanting something in return. You shall learn how to maintain conscious innocence."

"How is it possible for innocence to be conscious?"

"Isn't that a bitch?" replies Say When Daddy, applying a tourniquet to his wounded foot.

"Is not that a bitch?" repeats young Tongue Fu....

"Because of the length of my tongue," he is now telling his mother what he didn't tell the hot chestnuts vendor, "I have had to learn to speak very carefully. So that it will not show."

"My only obligation is to explain the circumstances which brought about your abnormal tongue. I promised your father that, before I left Japan. During World War Two, he was a volunteer Kamikaze pilot. They had all been trained in mysticism. It was necessary for them not to be concerned about death. Not when the premeditated loss of their own lives—in the process of destroying an American aircraft carrier—would save so many other Japanese lives.

"However, in 1945, there were those among their leaders preparing to surrender. Nevertheless, Japanese intelligence agents discovered that the United States had so much invested in developing the atomic bombs that they had to be dropped. Say When Daddy's suicide mission was intended to prevent those planes from ever taking off. But his own plane was shot down first.

"He survived, except for his eyesight. His flying goggles had melted into his eyeballs. I was an Air Force nurse at the time, and I happened to be assigned to his case. He was so ashamed to find himself alive in an enemy hospital that *hara-kiri* seemed to be his only alternative.

"Well, it was as though I had become a personification of the life force, overshadowing even the urge of his spiritual conditioning. And so you were conceived one night in an American hospital somewhere between Hiroshima and Nagasaki."

The teakettle boiling on the stove whistles at such a high pitch that one of the teacups breaks. Tongue Fu's mother pours the tea into two other cups.

"Nine months later," she sighs with tortured regret, "I was nursing you for the first time. And your tongue ... *unreeled* ... around my nipple. I went into shock. The doctors said your condition was a result of atomic fallout affecting the genes.

"Forgive me, my son, but I had to flee. I just couldn't bear to suckle even a second time this ... *freak. So* I left you with your father in a monastery.

"I returned here. Met a nice man. Got married. Gave birth to a normal daughter. Eventually got divorced ... and am settled in my life. I work at a hospital; I have my friends.

"The last I heard of your half-sister, she was pregnant and unmarried, in that order. We don't have much contact. She's a disciple of some guru. Here's her picture. Now please go. It's the kindest thing you can do."

In a slight state of confusion, Tongue Fu wanders along Broadway.

He goes into a dilapidated arcade with a sign in front that says AMUSEMENT CENTER. He stumbles past the mechanical Gypsy Lady in an isolation booth waiting to tell his fortune. Past the steering wheel that would permit him to drive down an obstacle-filled revolving road. Past the machine that he could stand on to have his feet vibrated. Past the miniature hockey game. Past the little metal prize-fighters ready to go into action at the drop of a coin.

He finally stops at an anti-aircraft gun. Faded lettering invites him to *Bomb the Japs Off the Map!* "Not still," he mumbles and walks out determinedly. Chinning himself easily up over the entrance, with his tongue snapping out again and again like a secret organic weapon, he selectively destroys certain letters in the word AMUSEMENT so that now the sign in front reads SEMEN CENTER.

In the window, a display of rubber masks resembling show-business and political celebrities all stare unseeingly at the strangeness of his performance, with the exception of Jacqueline Kennedy Onassis, who winks at him.

3

The Development of a New Friendship

The abandoned newsstand where Captain Mediafreak lives is furnished sparsely: color TV set; AM-FM radio; hi-fi stereo, records and earphones; tape recorder; photography equipment; motion-picture camera, tripod and cans of film; stacks of newspapers, magazines and underground comic books, including complete collections of *Zap* and *Slow Death.*

Plus a telephone, which he uses mostly to call up radio talk shows, which is what he is in the middle of doing at the moment.

"So the reason I'm against all censorship is that it's diametrically opposed to the essential purpose of education. People have to be allowed to make up their own minds."

"All right, thank you, caller," a professional voice interrupts. "Appreciate your point of view."

Captain Mediafreak hangs up, dials the same number and is put on hold. When he goes on the air again, he uses a different voice, somewhat nasal in quality.

"I'd like to disagree with that previous gentleman. I'm for censorship. My wife uses the television as a babysitter, you know, and there's an awful lot of violence. Our children are beginning to take all the violence for granted, and there are virtually no options. That's not entertainment, it's brainwashing. And in my opinion, brainwashing should be censored...."

FLASHICBACKIC:

Young Lieutenant Mediafreak has all of his arms and legs. His curly hairlocks are shorter. He sits in the front row of a movie theater, watching his first Andy Warhol film. It is called *Audience,* and consists entirely of hidden-camera panning leisurely over reactions of people in each audience waiting for the scene on the screen to change. Therefore it's different at every showing.

When he sees himself, Lieutenant Mediafreak immediately opens his guitar case and takes out a battery-operated electric saw. He proceeds to saw off his left leg, hearing himself scream in utter pain, as surrounding faces on the screen express their encouragement.

"Right on!" the audience yells.

Then his right leg.

"Right off!" the audience yells.

Then his left arm. "Right arm!" the audience yells.

Lieutenant Mediafreak faints. The electric saw falls on the ground, further dismembering the bloody limbs already lying there as though it were in heat.

An usher calls the police. The police call the newspapers.

The New York Daily News headline:

SELF-MUTILATOR DENIES IT WAS A DRUG FREAKOUT

The New York Times headline:

PERPETRATOR OF PUBLIC MASOCHISM
CLAIMS ARTISTIC STATEMENT WAS
ONLY INTENTION

The New York Post headline:

MOVIE VICTIM SUES WARHOL
FOR INVASION OF PRIVACY

It never occurs to Harry Reasoner that while he is delivering his Commentary on *The ABC Evening News*, Captain Mediafreak is initiating his house guest into the rite of cannabis-sharing.

Tongue Fu inhales the smoke carefully; coats his lungs with resin; then, in the very act of exhaling, gently passes the joint, which he holds, not between his fingers, but curled in the tip of his long parched tongue.

That night they decide to go out for dinner and the theater to celebrate their new friendship. Tongue Fu carries the basket from which Captain Mediafreak navigates their course. They arrive at an elegant hotel on Park Avenue.

Since they are the only ones in the elevator, Tongue Fu takes the liberty of pressing the button for the seventeenth floor with his tongue. As the numbers light up, he counts out loud: "... nine ... ten ... eleven ... twelve ... fourteen—where is thirteen?"

"Listen, there's a lot of places—office buildings, apartment houses, hotels—where they had the architect skip the thirteenth floor because it's supposed to be bad luck. There's even airplanes where they don't have a number thirteen seat. It's the same principle. They don't wanna lose any business. They're just catering to superstitious people, is all. The worst part of it is, the people who live on the fourteenth floor—they think they're getting away with it.

Walking along the corridor, they stop at a door that has a cart in front of it, containing a pair of trays with leftover food from Room Service. They share these mostly-eaten delicacies in the stairwell. Dessert is found on the floor below.

Then they depart for the theater, where a revival of *No, No, Nanette* is playing. They wait outside until the first act intermission. Mingling with the audience in the lobby, they return inside for the second act, finding an available seat in the balcony. Tongue Fu holds the basket on his lap.

"Why do they call it legitimate theater?" he asks on the way home. "Is there such a thing as illegitimate theater?"

"Absolutely," replies Captain Mediafreak. "Real life. Or maybe the movies."

"I have never been to a movie."

"You oughta see *Deep Throat*. Some people say *that's* illegitimate."

"I have heard the phrase. Other boys at the monastery in Japan used to whisper about *deep throat* as a very specialized form of yoga."

They stop to watch a potato-knish maker. His style strikes Tongue Fu as being more mellow than the pizza maker, perhaps because his task is less hectic.

A wizened panhandler straggles by and sputters, "Can ya spare a quarter for a Pina Colada?"

"I am sorry, but I do not have money. But come join us. Regard the potato-knish maker aiding the potato to achieve knishhood."

"Aw, never mind," says the panhandler, only to be replaced by a neatly-suited thin black man wearing a fedora and politely offering to sell a copy of *Muhammad Speaks*.

From his basket, Captain Mediafreak pipes up: "No, thanks. I'm already a subscriber."

4

Linda Lovelace Serves as a Catalyst

A doorbell chimes the first six notes ("They asked me how I knew . . .") of *Smoke Gets In Your Eyes.*

Chocolate Graham hums the next five notes ("... my true love was true"). She is twenty-three years old. She stands exactly four feet tall, but she is wearing platform shoes. Her skin is brown. Her head, with its close natural hairdo, bounces like licorice cotton candy as she skips like a child to answer the door.

A periscope arrangement enables her to look through the peephole. A special doorknob installed two feet off the ground enables her to open the door.

A deliveryperson hands her a box. "Oh, good. My new calling cards. I'd just about run out of them."

One of the cards is glued to the outside of the box. A rainbow reaches from one lower corner of the card to the other. Another rainbow, upside-down and interlocking with the first rainbow, reaches from one upper corner to the other. Fancy embossed lettering reads:

Can You Pass the CRAP Test?

Below, in tiny type, there's a telephone number.

The deliveryperson asks, "What's this crap test anyhow?"

"It's sort of a private joke."

"Well, I mean, whatdaya do with the cards? Are you in some kinda *business?*"

"No, it's more like a hobby. I just give them to certain people when they're not looking."

"No offense, ma'am, but you could slip 'em in their *pocket,* and they wouldn't even know the difference."

"That's exactly what I do, sometimes."

"I mean because you're the right height, y'know what I mean? Remember Johnny the bellhop, he used to go"—the delivery person cups his hands to his mouth and bellows in a falsetto voice—*"Call for Philip Morris! Call for Phillip Morris!*—I dunno if he was a dwarf or a midget, I can never tell the difference, not that I hafta tell the difference that often. Which are you, by the way? I mean I hope you don't mind my asking."

"Oh, that's okay. I'm not a dwarf *or* a midget. I'm a pygmy...."

FLASHI₢BACKI₢:

Young Chocolate Greystoke's hair is twisted into many mini-pigtails, each tied with a bright red ribbon. She is sitting in the parlor of her parents' mansion. They are an elderly Caucasian couple.

Mother: **"Chocolate, we've decided that the time has come to tell you that you were not actually *born* to us."**

Father: **"The truth of the matter is, we kidnapped you."**

Mother: "You must understand, your father was an orphan himself."

Father: "Yes, my parents were killed in a plane crash in an African jungle. However, the body of my younger brother—you've seen baby pictures of Uncle Tarzan in the family album—was not found among the wreckage."

Mother: "So we eventually went on a personal pilgrimage and, to make a long story short, we *took you.*"

Father: "I considered it a case of retroactive cultural exchange."

Mother: "But, Chocolate, we want you to know that we love you just as much as if you had been legally adopted...."

It's Saturday evening at the old abandoned newsstand.

"Do you desire," Tongue Fu asks Captain Mediafreak, "to go see a movie?"

"Nah, you better go alone. This is family night for me. I'll give you some cash, though. They don't have intermission at films."

"Where is your family?"

"Right here." With his one and only hand, Captain Mediafreak gestures toward his TV set. "The Bunkers at eight o'clock—Archie and Edith and Michael and Gloria and their neighbors—and then at eight-thirty there's *M.A.S.H.*, with Hawkeye, Trapper, Hot Lips, Radar and all *their* gang."

"These names do not mean anything to me."

"Yeah, well, I'm closer to them than to my own flesh-and-blood family, I'll tell you that. And at 9 o'clock there's Mary Tyler Moore, and Rhoda and Lou Grant and Ted Baxter. I'd really miss them if I went a whole Saturday night without seeing any of 'em."

"But is it not odd that your pleasure should come from watching other people live their lives for you?"

"Listen, it's not even other people. It's actors *pretending to be* other people. But, like, at 9:30 there's Bob Newhart and those other characters on his show—they're more fun than most of the real people I know. And then at 10, it's Carol Burnett, with Harvey Korman and Vicki Lawrence and Lyle Waggoner and Tim Conway—I consider them family— they're delightful compared to my actual relatives.

I mean, the *Tonight Show* is like going to a party every night, and you don't even have to do anything. I'd rather watch Johnny Carson than go to a party and listen to people talk about what he said in his opening monologue on the previous night. And I really love spectator conversation. You don't have to keep responding to anyone. I even watch re-runs of talk shows. You'd be surprised how much you miss the first time around."

And so Tongue Fu goes to see *Deep Throat* by himself.

On the screen, a gigantic close-up of Linda Lovelace is sucking away at an unidentified throbbing penis. For Tongue Fu, the fantasy of probing the recesses of her throat and sensuously rubbing her displaced clitoris to climax with his own unique tongue results in such a holy hard-on that he becomes convinced he has finally met his soulmate.

To inquire about her, he approaches the office of the theater manager, Buff Mogul, just as the police swoop in to arrest him for displaying an obscene film. Tongue Fu gets arrested along with him, as a material witness, because his erection won't detumesce. It remains aloft all the way to the precinct house.

PETE VON SHOLLY

An officer tells them, "You're each allowed to make one phone call."

Buff Mogul scratches one of his fresh sideburns while he talks to his attorney. Then he tells Tongue Fu, "Don't worry, my lawyer'll get us both out of here tonight."

"But I am allowed to make one phone call also."

Buff Mogul takes a card from the pocket of his mod jacket and passes it to Tongue Fu.

"Here," he says, "I have no idea where this came from. Why don't you try phoning and see what happens."

Tongue Fu looks at Chocolate Graham's calling card. Then he dials her number with the tip of his tongue.

5
A Date with Chocolate Graham

It's Sunday morning, and Captain Mediafreak is busy baking hash-oil cookies to eat during the telecast of a football game.

"You got yourself a blind date," he is saying to Tongue Fu, "that's what it sounds like to me."

"What is a blind date?"

"Well, first of all, a *date* is where you take a girl out to eat and to a movie and then you take 'er home and get laid. Traditionally speaking, that is. Of course, that doesn't apply to you because you've taken this vow of celibacy."

"I do not ever take a vow."

"Well, anyway, a *blind* date is where you've never seen each other before."

That afternoon, the first thing Tongue Fu says to Chocolate Graham is, "Would you like a hash-oil cookie?"

"How do you know I'm not a narcotics agent?"

"I do not know. You did not say on the telephone."

"Let me put it this way: How do I know *you're* not a narcotics agent?"

"I am not."

"Never mind. I'm just teasing. If the narcs are this subtle. I'll join 'em. Come on in." A couple-dozen folks of all ages are seated on cushions in her living room. When Tongue Fu gets comfortable, she begins to address the group....

FLASHBACKIE

Say When Daddy is presenting young Tongue Fu with a personalized volume of the *I Ching*.

"Keep this with you always, Anteater, and consult it for guidance whenever you are in doubt."

"But how can a book know anything about my activities?"

"Open it," the old man grins, "and it will open you."

Tongue Fu accepts the book and opens it. Instead of there being pages inside, up springs an Oriental jack-in-the-box holding a placard on a stick, bearing this message in calligraphy:

THERE IS ONLY NOW
AND THAT IS ALREADY GONE.

"There is only now," Tongue Fu whispers—"and that is already gone." Then out loud: "I vow to remember this message."

"No, Anteater, to make a vow is to not live in the present. It is to postpone your strength. You must *develop* your strength, moment by moment."

He takes a handful of marbles from his pocket and slowly tosses them, one after another, into the air toward young Tongue Fu, who in turn catches each marble by balancing it on the end of his tongue, which darts up with amazing accuracy.

"Ah, Anteater, how many hearts will you break with that tongue of yours? Cunnilingus would never be the same after you."

"I do not wish to hurt anyone. I shall abstain from such gratification of the flesh."

"So soon you are trying to live in the future?"

"You are right, Master. I will take no more vows."

"Do you know, Anteater, what is the sound of one hand clapping?"

"Is there a correct answer to such a question?"

"Do not attempt to find it yet. Some day you will meet your mother and you will learn why it is that only through the grace of hundreds of thousands of dead souls do you experience the ecstasy of existence. That's the way the satori bounces."

"That is the way the satori bounces...."

"All right now, just to conclude my rap before I answer your questions," Chocolate Graham is saying. "I ought to explain what the CRAP Test is. The initials stand for *Coincidence Rationalization and Practice.* That's my working philosophy.

"It's one thing to accept the myriad of coincidences that started governing your life before you were even born—how your parents met, how their parents met, and then the inconceivable coincidence of a specific spermatozoan and ovum uniting to culminate in each of us—but it's another thing to set about deliberately *arranging coincidences.*

"Every one of you is here today because of the coincidence of time and space which allowed me to slip you my card. But then you screened yourselves in as a function of your own curiosity.

"Now, I've read ten thousand books—I'm not exaggerating; if a footnote turned me on, I would seek out the book it referred to—and when I try to summarize all the wisdom I've synthesized, it boils down on one level to the arbitrariness of institutions, in every civilization.

"We, as humans, are the only species that wars with itself in so many ways, because we're the only species that can *conceptualize* its own destruction. Which means if enough of us change our own personal direction—by exercising our power of choice to the fullest extent—then alternative *positive* institutions will evolve.

"Two years ago I used a portion of my trust fund to purchase a large chunk of land in Oregon, and this summer it will become Camp Crap, dedicated to the celebration of consciousness. Spiritual leaders from all over the world will participate on a continuing basis, but that's a mutual con game, because I believe we're all capable of spreading influence.

"Just how we go about doing that will be probed at individual meetings. The only cost will be the dime you've already spent to phone me in the first place. Okay. Are there any questions?"

The first question comes from the man who delivered her calling cards the previous day.

"What I'd like to know is, how do you know which people to give your cards to?"

"Yes, well, being a pygmy has been of great help. In this country, the mere sight of me indicates that I'm a member of three oppressed classes: I'm a little person; I'm a person of color; and I'm a person of the female persuasion. I am a triple invisible. And I have rolled *with* that actuality. I'm also bisexual, but that doesn't show. It has to *show* to help them treat you invisibly. So, to answer your question, the basis on which I choose people to give cards to is, essentially, I eavesdrop on their vibes."

PETE VON SHOLLY

6

Tongue Fu Becomes
a Fellow Traveler

Captain Mediafreak and Tongue Fu decide to make a few extremely low-budget film shorts.

On Monday, they shoot *Community Control,* following an ant carrying another ant on its back along the sidewalk, with a record of *He's Not Heavy, He's My Brother* serving as the soundtrack.

On Tuesday, they shoot *Counter Clockwise,* capturing a group of pre-teenagers on the Carousel in Central Park, passing around a joint as their painted horses slide up and down.

On Wednesday, they shoot *Energy Crisis,* immortalizing the sales pitch for a portable electric artificial vagina in a novelty items store.

The next day, Chocolate Graham keeps her appointment at the film partners' abandoned newsstand. She joins in on their cannabis-sharing rite while the TV news is on.

Walter Cronkite finishes delivering the weekly war dead statistics when Captain Mediafreak suddenly snaps his fingers and says, "It's the body count—today must be *Thursday*—who wants to take some acid with me?"

All three swallow their LSD tablets with the aid of peach-flavored kefir, while Eric Sevareid gives his official opinion of an upcoming space mission: "A celestial challenge...."

"I could do news analysis," Captain Mediafreak says. "Look how they never show the bottom half of his body. They could just place me right on top of the desk."

"With all the television you watch," Chocolate Graham asks, "what would you say is the most significant pattern you've observed?"

"I'd say," Captain Mediafreak ponders her question. "the tendency to divide people of different backgrounds, under the pretense of bringing them together."

"But what about the infiltration of counter-values?"

"It's pretty schizy. Susan Saint James will go on the Merv Griffin show and talk about the importance of being a vegetarian, but then she'll be on *McMillan and Wife* and order a steak dinner. Or Blythe Danner'll tell a *TV Guide* interviewer that she doesn't wear any makeup, but then she'll wear makeup on *Adam's Rib,* which ironically is supposed to be about a liberated woman."

"And, finally," Walter Cronkite is saying, "CBS learned today that the late Judy Garland had a clause in her will requesting that the makeup man from *Green Acres* be hired to apply the cosmetics to her face while her body lies in state. In Hollywood, however, Eva Gabor, star of the situation comedy, refused to grant him a leave of absence. And that's the way it is."

"And that is the way it is," repeats Tongue Fu.

He takes out his kazoo and evokes from it a calming high-pitched melody.

Chocolate Graham listens for a while, then says "Only an ordained Patoonga priest could play a kazoo like that. May I see your belly-button?"

Tongue Fu takes off his shirt.

Chocolate Graham stares at his bellybutton, which stares unceasingly back at her...."

FLASHI€BACKI€:

Luke Warm Sake is tattooing a third eye on the bellybutton of post-adolescent Tongue Fu, whose shaved head is betrayed by a five o'clock shadow.

"Ah, yes, Anteater, bellybuttons are what we all have in common, yet no two are alike, as with snowflakes and fingerprints. Bellybuttons are my specialty, but once I tattooed everything from a ladybug on a lady's thigh to a pornographic mural on a gentleman's entire body.

"During the war I was taken prisoner and coerced into decorating the bodies of my captors. One officer insisted that I perform a tattoo on the space between his lips and his nose. I had to be extremely careful with the needle. He forced me to inscribe *Fuck the Japs* there above his upper lip. Perhaps he has since grown a mustache.

"Ah, there we are, Anteater, all finished. As a Patoonga priest, I have rendered you separate but equal. That did not hurt as much as your anticipation, did it? Remember to contemplate the illusion of pain, and it will disappear as easily as removing lint from your third eye...."

Chocolate Graham is dancing to the beat of Aretha Franklin singing *Respect*.

When the record ends, she asks Tongue Fu, "Shall I show you what the sound of one hand clapping is?"

With an intensely gradual approach, she moves her right hand until it comes to rest on his left cheek. He does the same to her. Then their hands glide into a spontaneous hugging.

The pair engulf Captain Mediafreak into their embrace. It is he who breaks the silence.

"You'll hafta excuse me now. I've gotta watch *The Waltons.*"

Tongue Fu seems perplexed. "Am I not supposed to follow the Waltons?"

"I checked the schedule. Your summer replacement starts tonight."

Chocolate Graham is removing her clothes. Tongue Fu does likewise.

And then, with neither one speaking a word, they begin to make love, each touch emanating from such total attention that it all appears to be happening in exquisite slow motion.

PETE VON SHOLLY

As Captain Mediafteak watches the Waltons finding joy in the Depression, Tongue Fu is going down on Chocolate Graham, and she is going up on him.

Now she is astride him, their genitals mingling in a maze of colors.

"There is only now," he struggles to say, as if to avoid becoming lost in the mounting tension, but his psyche yields to her uninhibited spasms with his own inevitable ejaculation, so that he can barely whisper in the soft afterglow, "and that's already gone."

Tongue Fu has had his first contraction.

Part Two

7

Introducing Rosebud Zwalyimeh

A Volkswagen gathering reduced speed on an Oregon country highway is entirely pasted over with little American flag decals. Only the windows, headlights, brake signals, license plates and door handles have been left uncovered. Also, the radio antenna is still bare, the better to pull in the sound waves of Van Morrison singing *Into the Mystic.*

The driver of this starred-and-striped vehicle is Rosebud Zwalyimeh. Long auburn hair parted in the middle shelters a face enhanced by an expression of amused awareness that its beauty is deemed so by Caucasian countercultural conditioning. She is wearing a see-through Mexican blouse and jeans embroidered with imaginary tropical fish.

Occasionaly she passes a roadside billboard. One announces a series of evangelical revival meetings in the area to be conducted by faith-healer Anal Roberts. Another features Smokey the Bear endorsing the Air Force Reserves. Another simply says, *Compliments of a Friend.*

Eventually, Rosebud picks up a hitchhiker—a uniformed highway patrol person.

"Don't you know it's against the law," he asks, "to stop on a public freeway like that?"

"But, officer—*you* were thumbing a ride."

"Well, I had to. Somebody stole my motorcycle."

"Are you going to give me a ticket?"

"Depends." He removes his helmet. "What is it with all those decals? You making fun of the American flag?"

"I thought that's supposed to be patriotic—to display—"

"One decal, sure. Two, maybe three. Five, even ten is still patriotic. But not the whole goddam *car.* That's ridiculous."

"At what point does it become unpatriotic, though?"

"I would say a dozen decals begins to border on sarcasm."

"Suppose I were a sweet little old lady; wouldn't you just consider it eccentric behavior?"

"Yeah, probably."

"Then tell me, at what age does sarcasm turn into eccentricity?"

"I give up," he says, pretending not to look at the outline of her bosom. "But the last time I tried to have a discussion with somebody dressed like you, she called me a pig."

"Because of something you did?"

"No, because of this uniform. I *was* actually a pig *before* I became a cop, but they cheered me for that...."

FLASHIEBACKIE:

A large crowd at a peace rally is cheering the highway patrol person, a few years younger, as he stands on a flatbed truck being used for a stage. He is wearing a uniform of the Green Berets, and holds up between his thumb and first two fingers, a detached human ear on the other side of the microphone into which he speaks.

"I appreciate your applause," he says to the audience, "but please remember that I'm really talking to this ear. Forgive me, ear, for cutting you off as a souvenir from one of my many victims."

Someone in the crowd calls out: " You're the victim! *You're* the victim!"

"Forgive me, ear, for having tortured your former owner and forcing you to listen to his screams of pain."

"It wasn't your fault," someone else shouts. "You were just a lackey for the ruling class!"

"Forgive me, ear, for shooting heroin so that I could drive shooting bullets out of my mind."

"It's all right," the ear responds. "You were already addicted to the system...."

Two shadowy figures are pouring gasoline over a third one who sits on a stolen highway patrol motorcycle. At dusk he rides it down a city street, turns onto the sidewalk, crashes straight through the plate glass window of the Chase-Folly Bank and proceeds to explode into fire.

The local newspaper receives this handwritten message:

> *Materialism has become obsolete.*
>
> *Spirituality continues to fill the void.*
>
> *Any inconvenience to citizens is a necessary by product of abstract complicity.*
>
> *We are all responsible for whatever the banks do with our money.*
>
> *What happened at Chase-Folly must be considered as the first American Kamikaze action.*
>
> *Heretofore, individuals have destroyed only themselves because they were too sensitive to bear inhumanity any longer.*
>
> *However, there has now come into being a new organization for those of us who wish to transform our acts of self-destruction into socially useful deeds.*
>
> *If you decide to take your own life, why not remove an evil institution in the process?*
>
> *That is the only requirement to join Better Your Exit.*
>
> *—BYE Communication #1*

Not too long after Rosebud Zwalyimeh drops off the highway patrol person at his attorney's office downtown, she picks up another hitchhiker. But this one isn't thumbing a ride, he's *tonguing* a ride.

"Where are you going?" Rosebud asks.

"I am working at Camp Crap," Tongue Fu answers. 'That's where I am headed for. Is not this an amazing coincidence?"

"Perhaps not. Must we not also contemplate all those coincidences which do *not* happen to us?"

8

Welcome to Camp Crap

They're all over the place. Gurus. Each one wears a sweatshirt that says CRAP on the front, in order to distinguish them from amateurs, disciples, skeptics, tourists, reporters and concessionaires.

The paths to consciousness are paved with stalls, tents, booths, domes, teepees, trailers and huts.

A group of Rosicrucians and a group of Freemasons are engaging in a tug-of-war without a rope.

Chocolate Graham is touching the thigh of a swami with a purple turban.

"No," he says, "you must not do that. We should

abstain from such pleasures of the flesh since it is all an illusion anyway so why bother ourselves, you see?"

"Testing. One, two, three. Testing." This voice is coming from a speaker system beside a gigantic television screen set up in the middle of a field. In the woods there is an outhouse with a sign nailed to the door that reads *TV Ching.*

An audience of a few hundred watches an image begin to form on the screen. It's a naked man standing next to a two-seater toilet.

"Are we on? Lovely. Good afternoon. I represent the Asshole Liberation Front. Our premise is that any level of illumination must be able to withstand the temporal indignity of defecation or it isn't worth being communicated. In my own case, of course, they're inseparable."

He stands on one of the toilet seats, then squats. As he squeezes out a turd, his face grimaces with delight.

A Spanish-speaking couple strolls onto the field just in time to witness this display on *TV Ching.*

"Mira, mira,—esta el Phil Donahue Show!

"Si, si,—aldes uno de los Moonies!"

"Sometimes I think my bowels move me more than I move them. I tell you, my friends, this is basic. There's a one-way mirror in here, with a television camera behind it, but my demonstration should be on all the *networks.* Oh, I realize it might seem trivial, but the importance of squatting cannot be exaggerated."

A pair of federal agents is busy taking notes. One, Primo Colombian of the FBI, is wearing a new pre-soiled trench coat. The other, Notary Sojak of the CIA, is wearing a completely shaved head...."

FLASHI€BACKI€:

The Chief Coordinator is giving instructions to Colombian and Sojak.

"What we want to do is link up the Camp Crap people with the Better Your Exit group. Now, our surveillance indicates that there's a half-Japanese fellow at the camp whose father was a Kamikaze pilot in World War Two. With a tie-in like that, he would be a particularly relevant target of your investigation."

Colombian: "Lemme ask ya somethin', Chief. How we gonna prove these people are subversive if they're operating right out in the open?"

Sojak: "I'll answer that. They're shrewd. They don't wanna look suspicious. That's the most suspicious thing about them."

Colombian: "Well, I been readin' a book of Haiku poetry so I can start a casual conversation with the Japanese guy. They all have to be seventeen syllables."

Sojak: "I don't know about your style, Colombian. I prefer the straight forward approach. I'm not dumb, and I'm not gonna *pretend* to be dumb."

Colombian: "It's just a way of learnin' stuff, Sojak. I even started writin' one of them little poems. Listen to this. I call it 'Haiku with Five Syllables Missing.'"

He takes a scrap of paper from his pocket and reads aloud:

**We stayed up all night
Discussing the sense
Of touch....**

❀

Rosebud Zwalyimeh is touching the same thigh of that same swami with the purple turban.

"Yes," he says, "you must do that. We should not abstain from such pleasures of the flesh since it is all an illusion anyway so why not indulge ourselves, you see?"

"But then why did you reject my friend, Chocolate?"

"She is not nearly so beautiful as you."

'Why, you're nothing but a Superficial Chauvinist!" She withdraws her hand. "Don't you think there's a passion inside *her* little body too?"

The swami puts his hand on her thigh. She removes it.

"Does this mean," he asks, "that you have come here only to test my consistency?"

"That's right, swami. It's a technique we used successfully in the civil rights movement. A black person would try to rent a home and be told it wasn't available. Then a white person would try, and if it turned out to be available, legal action could be taken."

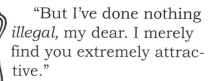

"But I've done nothing *illegal,* my dear. I merely find you extremely attractive."

"Well, you can just take your turban and shove it up your purple illusion."

PETE von STOLLY

9

The Scientologeek and the Frankfurter Maker

"Crap," is how Captain Mediafreak answers the camp phone. He's in charge of the switchboard.

"Yeah, this is me ... Hey, Mom, how ya doin'? ... Are you kidding? They started the summer re-runs in the spring.... Well, I'll tell ya, my TV was always warmed up, even when it wasn't on—which means the power was going twenty-four hours a day—and one night I caught myself switching on the set and realizing the utter absurdity of saving a few seconds before a program about the energy shortage came on—sponsored by an oil company, yet—so I just decided to give it all up and come out here. Besides, Tongue Fu was beginning to get hooked on the tube.... He's out getting me a hot dog right now...."

Waiting on the line leading to a frankfurter stand, Tongue Fu is showing the photograph of his half-sister to a follower of Scientologeek standing in front of him, who doesn't recognize her, but takes out a photo himself.

"This was my brother. He's the one who supposedly drove that motorcycle into the bank. But I absolutely don't believe he killed himself. We talked about suicide once—just an intellectual discussion—and he said he would never consider it because he preferred to shun irrevocable decisions. I think he must've been hypnotized by the Communists."

He is holding an empty soup can in each hand. They're attached by wires to a Geek-Meter, which he glances at while he speaks.

"Oh, good," he notes. "I'm telling the truth again."

When he reaches the front of the line, the Scientologeek requests, "One hot dog, please "—holding up his index finger in a gesture indicating *one,* which he is convinced must have originated with cave dwellers—"and could you make it well done?"

The frankfurter maker takes the hot dog that's closest to him on the rotating machine and sticks it inside a roll.

"Excuse me, I asked for well done."

"This is well done. Show me one that's well done."

"There." The Scientologeek points toward a hot dog that appears well done. "That one."

"All right," the frankfurter maker snarls, "you want that one, I'll give you that one, but it's raw."

"Never mind. I'll take the one you already fixed up."

"Look, you ignorant bastard, I've been cooking hot dogs on this machine for *ten years!*"

The Scientologeek stands there, the eternal customer, thinking: *Where's the manager? I'm going to call the manager!*

The frankfurter maker stands there, the eternal merchant, thinking: *How many times do I have to tell you? Ain't you never gonna learn?*

The Scientologeek checks his Geek-Meter to determine the validity of his emotion....

FLASHIЄBACKIЄ:

At a Scientologeek church meeting, the minister is concluding his sermon to a congregation of smiling faces.

"And so it is important, in understanding unhappiness on the job, to be cognizant of the fact that an individual who relates to the universe through a machine has a tendency, first to imitate the *motion* of that machine; then to become assimilated with the *content* of that machine; and finally to become virtually *subservient* to that machine. It becomes an object of worship, and justifiably so.

"The machine is a central clearing house for the basic needs of that worker. It provides him with a source of income. It provides him with a circle of like-minded companions. But most of all, it provides him with an unbounded objectivity which renders subjective praise of the machine itself unto a state of clear contradiction.

"But it *functions*...."

Tongue Fu orders, "One hot dog with everything on it, please. And a large Payola-Cola."

The frankfurter maker grasps at a straw and pulls the proper spigot.

On his way back to the office where Captain Mediafreak is waiting, Tongue Fu sees Rosebud Zwalyimeh, and they walk there together, arms linking. He tells her about his encounter with the Scientologeek.

"Self-hypnotism," says Rosebud. "That's what this whole camp is *really* all about. It's a transformation of the cultural programming toward romance, where you keep focusing on the image of the person you're infatuated with. Only now, instead of a sexual object, there's a constant refocusing on the guru of your choice."

"I do not need a Geek-Meter," says Tongue Fu, "to tell me that I love you."

"You know," sighs Rosebud, "I was raped a few years ago by a dude who said 'I love you' just before he came. And those words have never been the same to me. So just put your sweet tongue in my ear and you don't have to say anything. I'll know."

Without losing step or moving his head any closer to hers—relying entirely on peripheral vision—he places his tongue comfortably in her ear, and they continue walking.

A television cameraperson approaches them, film rolling. Tongue Fu whips his tongue out of Rosebud's ear with almost invisible swiftness, and with it he turns the camera around one hundred eighty degrees so that the lens is looking back over the cameraperson's shoulder, and then just as swiftly Tongue Fu returns his tongue to Rosebud's ear.

"Ooh, that felt good," she says. "Do it again."

Tongue Fu removes his tongue from Rosebud's ear but instead of returning it he explains his act: "The camera saw my tongue in your ear but out of context."

"Can't you keep talking while your tongue is still in my ear, just like they do when they kiss in the comic books?"

He tries, but his words are inaudible.

When they reach the office, Captain Mediafreak says, "My mother sends her regards."

A radio bulletin announces: "Another development in the Better Your Exit Kamikaze case. Police say they have discovered a mysterious Oriental ear in the debris at the Chase-Folly Bank. Further details concerning this latest clue on the 6 o'clock news."

The telephone rings.

Rosebud says to Tongue Fu, "If you think my ear would be out of context—"

Captain Mediafreak picks up the phone and says, "Bullshit. I mean Crap."

10

An Evening
with *TV Ching*

The season progresses. Thousands of
blankets with families and friends are now sprawled
on the field simultaneously watching *TV Ching* and
the sun setting pink and grey behind it.

On the gigantic screen, FBI agent Primo Colombian and CIA agent Notary Sojak are sitting on the
twin toilets, talking to each other. Nailed to the wall
behind them is a plaque that reads:

> *"Refresh my bowels*
> *in the Lord. "*
>
> *—St. Paul, Philemon 1:20*

Colombian: "Well, we have undercover children
working the Pen Pal circuit now. My own kid is
corresponding with a Black Panther kid to find out
what their free breakfast program is really a front
for."

Sojak: "Great. And we have counterfeit one-dollar
bills flooding the country. The lines at banks and
stores are moving like molasses, because it takes so
much time to check'em out. Not like your counter-

feit twenty-dollar bills. This is much more equitable. *Any*body can get stuck with singles. We'll *see* what happens when the wealth is spread around. Chaos, that's what."

There is a sudden knock on the door, followed by a female voice saying, "Hello in there?"

A duet: "Who's there?"

"My name is Innocence." She sticks her frizzied-head in the door and continues. "I'm sorry to disturb you gentlemen, but are you aware that you're on *TV Ching;,*"

"What?" says Colombian. "You mean this is the outhouse where all that philosophical stuff comes from?"

Sojak turns toward the one-way mirror and confides: "He's only kidding, folks. Always pretending to be dumb—that's his *style,* y'know. The truth is, *of course* we know we're being watched. Twice a day. But I for one am proud to say that only in America could your protectors afford to be so arrogant. And I know that goes for my partner, too—right, Colombian?"

"Huh? Oh, sure. Say, listen, Sojak, I've been workin' on that Haiku."

He reaches down to his pants, which are crumpled on the floor surrounding his shoes, takes a scrap of paper out of a pocket, and reads:

We stayed up all night
Discussing the sense
Of touch . . .
At sunrise we fucked.

"Now," muses Colombian, "I just gotta work out the line structure."

"C'mon, let's get outa here before you blow our cover," says Sojak, buckling his belt and practicing his laugh.

Innocence takes their place on the *TV Ching*.

"I liked it better with five syllables missing," she begins. "But seriously, I would just like to say a few words. Live your alternative. Thank you."

In the field there is scattered applause as Innocence departs and Tongue Fu enters.

"I am looking for my sister," he says, holding her photograph up to the one-way mirror. "Perhaps one of you has seen her."

Tongue Fu is replaced on *TV Ching* by a Cowboy in his sixties. He places toilet tissue on the seat before he permits his buttocks to come in contact with it.

"I understand that CRAP is an acronym for *Coincidence Rationalization and Practice*. Well, that sounds anti-religious to me. I'm here to tell you folks about the greatest coincidence that ever happened to me...."

FLASHIEBACKIE:

The Cowboy in his forties is standing in front of a saloon. A Yankee of the same age bracket is standing across the street in front of the general store. Each has a holster on his hip.

They move clockwise, with all deliberate slowness, step by bowlegged step, until they are finally facing each other down the middle of the street.

Spectators lined up on both sides observe in silence. An Indian removes a feather from the base of his braid. The Cowboy says to the Yankee: "You are betraying the American Dream."

The Yankee says to the Cowboy: " You are betraying the American Dream."

The Indian says: "The American Dream was a Nightmare"—and tosses his feather high up into the air. Tension permeates the atmosphere. The feather drifts back and forth, lower and lower. An anonymous harmonica player does a bluesy version of *That Old Black Magic*.

When the feather finally touches the ground, both the Cowboy and the Yankee simultaneously reach for their guns and shoot all in the same motion.

The two bullets travel toward their respective targets, but meet, instead, midway between the Cowboy and the Yankee, in a head-on collision. They explode into each other with such fury that they create, while suspended in mid-air, the most expensive coin in the world....

"And it's still enshrined in the National Archives," says the old Cowboy, wiping away pieces of feces from his wrinkled tushy. "Strange. We wear our fake jewelry and keep our precious jewels in a safe. But you can never tell me that the coincidence of this shoot-out incident was not personally ordained by the Almighty!"

The Cowboy is followed by a middle-aged man who announces: "I've decided to come out of the closet right here on *TV Ching*. There's no reason why I should hide my homosexuality any longer. The reason the government is against Gay Liberation is because they can't blackmail us unless we're ashamed of it...."

When he departs, a young man with a new beard and shaggy hair takes his place.

"I'm a veteran," he says, "and I have some good news and some bad news. First, the good news: We can finally pull out our ground forces and end the war. The bad news is the reason why: Because, now that there's a new distribution setup for our opium supply, we won't need all those returning G.I. cadavers any more."

Rosebud Zwalyimeh, watching *TV Ching* in the field, blurts out to herself, "I know who that is." She runs to catch him leaving the outhouse.

"I recognize you," she breathes heavily. "You're Officer Serpento. Remember me—Rosebud? I signed an affidavit in your lawyer's office that I gave you a ride when your motorcycle was stolen. What are you doing out of uniform?"

"Oh, well, I left the force so I could devote full time to organizing."

"But why do you allow the media to continue circulating that phony Oriental ear story? There's no mystery. It belonged to you."

"You better forget about that. It was a stupid mistake. I should never have left it in my tool kit. But you've got to understand. That ear was like my credentials for infiltrating the Rotten Apples—that's a vigilante organization, consisting of one bad cop from every precinct—but I need a different image now. Don't look, but we're being watched by a couple of Feds."

Rosebud looks anyway. Colombian waves at her. Sojak kicks him in the ankle.

"How do you like my earring?" Serpento asks. "I even got myself pierced for the cause. You've got to trust me."

11
Visit to a Nude Exorcist Parlor

"I'd like you to check out that nude exorcist parlor," Chocolate Graham is saying. "Make sure it's not a front for prostitution. That could be used to discredit us."

And so Tongue Fu wanders toward the area of Camp Crap that has come to be known as Participation Valley.

There is a makeshift solitary confinement cell in which a former prisoner teaches his method of Enforced Meditation for twenty-three-and-a-half hours a day.

Further down, there is a continuing experiment on the effect of conflicting prayer upon plants. For couples only. A middle-aged wife and husband take turns pleading before a row of tomato plants.

She: "Please, God, let these luscious plants grow!"

He: "No, *don't* grow, you lousy red bitches!"

She: "Give them nourishment, oh Lord above!"

He: Wither and die, you little mothers!"

She: "Hear me, Jehovah, protect these little beings to survive on their native American soil!"

He: "Go back into the dirt, you filthy pinko, greenies!"

She: "Give them strength through photosynthesis, I beseech you!"

He: "Kill! Kill! Kill!"

Tongue Fu watches with weary preoccupation, then moves on to a shack decorated all over with Persian bedspreads. Standing in front, wearing a nun's outfit, is Virginia Real, fingering her rosary beads.

"Would you like to have a nude exorcism? Only ten cents a minute. Come on in, take your clothes off and get rid of whatever evil thoughts possess you...."

FLASHIEBACKIE:

Young Virginia Real, wearing a pressed convent school uniform, sits on one side of a confessional booth, twisting her flame-red hair.

"I let a boy feel my tits last night."

"Breasts," the priest on the other side corrects her. "Tits are vulgar."

"My breasts. First the left one. Then the right one. Then both together. Then just the left one again. Then—"

"You mustn't permit a representative of the devil to take advantage of your body, my child. That is a privilege which has to be *earned*.

"But why does God make it feel so *nice* then?"

"Allow me to quote from the Scriptures." He leafs through a Bible. "Here it is, *The Book of Job*. 'What?

Shall we receive good at the hand of God, and shall we not receive evil?"'"

"I've read that too, Father, and it seems to me that God tosses out good and evil arbitrarily, just because Satan *taunts* him into it."

"God was testing Job's faith."

"Well, I think God's on a terrible ego trip then."

"For shame. For shame."

"If I were God, I would've just let Job alone."

"Please, we're getting off the subject. Now, you say it felt nice for this boy to feel your breasts. But your guilt doesn't feel so nice, eh?..."

Tongue Fu has removed his clothes. So has Virginia Real. They sit naked on facing chairs.

"Love your third eye," she says.

"You have pink pubic hair," he observes.

"Yes, I know. Now tell me, exactly what would you like to have exorcised? Don't be shy."

"I want to know—I am wondering if—you are a—prostitute?"

"Ah, I understand what's troubling you." She takes a deep breath, clasps her hands and moves her lips in a silent prayer that gradually becomes audible. "Begone, oh demon of commerce!... Free this victim of your mercenary ways!... Cast out thy exploitative self from this walking prison!..."

After ten solid minutes of being harangued in such fashion, Tongue Fu asks her to stop.

"I feel," he says, "as though I am being turned into a human tomato plant."

Virginia Real glances at her clock. "You owe me one dollar. Look, I'm not a hooker, but I *do* think you're kinda cute. Would you like to ball or anything? No charge."

"I would be grateful," he hesitates, "if you would massage—my tongue."

He moistens a dollar bill with the tip of his tongue, leaves it sticking there and passes it to her that way.

"Holy muscle!... Would you"—she hesitates—"whip me—with your tongue?"

"I do not wish to inflict pain."

"Oh, please. You'll be inflicting pain if you *don't*. *I'll* give you your dollar back if you do it."

"But that would make me a prostitute."

"I'll tell you what. I'll massage your tongue if you'll whip me with it."

"But," he is obviously tempted, "would that not be prostituting my tongue?"

"Think of it as barter," she says, limbering up her fingers.

As if in belated response to the Jackie Kennedy rubber mask in that Times Square Amusement Center window, the third eye tattooed on Tongue Fu's bellybutton winks at Virginia Real while she whines with pleasure at each slimy lashing of his sacred tongue across her lower back.

12

Tongue Fu Meets His Sister

The Scientologeek recognizes Tongue Fu leaving a workshop in Advanced Breathing.

"Hey! That photo you showed me the other week. I saw her. She's with the Giggling Maharishi caravan over the hill there."

"Oonga-Boonga, Patoonga."

"I beg your pardon?"

"That is an ancient blessing of appreciation. I am a Patoonga priest."

"Beautiful. I thought you were a plainclothes cop looking for a runaway."

"I do not lie. She is my sister. I must go find her."

Over the hill, the Giggling Maharishi is in the middle of delivering a lecture on Transcendental Lactation to a group of disgruntled dairy industry conventioneers wearing *Milk Does Something to Every Body* lapel buttons.

"After all," he giggles, "statistics show that bottle-fed babies have a higher infant mortality rate." Giggle. "You Westerners are very anxious to export your artificial culture to underdeveloped nations, from the cradle to the casket." Giggle, giggle. "You send us bottles we cannot sterilize adequately, to fill with expensive formula that must be watered down so that we can afford it." Triumphant giggle. "But if you want a formula for *living,* I can give you that, as I have done with many famous people...."

FLASHI€BACKI€:

Back in the mountains of India, the Giggling Maharishi is listening patiently to the Beatles singing *Hey Jude* under a tree. When they get to the line, "Take a sad song," he stops them abruptly and says: "I demand to know why the four of you have decided to leave so suddenly, after all I have done for you."

John Lennon: "You're supposed to know everything. So why should we tell you?"

George Harrison: "Wait, I think we owe him an explanation."

Paul McCartney: "The truth is, we discovered that you gave each of us the exact same so-called individualized mantra."

Ringo Starr: "Of course, we had to betray your confidence in order to find that out."

PETE VON SHOLLY

The Giggling Maharishi angrily takes his portable tank of nitrous oxide and leaves, while the Beatles continue singing: "... and make it better...."

Tongue Fu sneaks around the grounds until he chances upon this pastoral scene: a couple of dozen females in their teens and twenties, all sitting quietly cross-legged in a large circle in the meadow, each simultaneously munching on a brownie, nursing a baby with one breast and pumping the other breast of its milk into a special container.

He recognizes his sister among them, but rather than interrupt, he walks slowly around their perimeter, playing a soothing melody on his kazoo. He then balances it on the tip of his tongue. Several of the women look up, smile and utter, "Far out." His tongue protrudes another few inches, and they utter, "Further out."

One by one, they get up and pour the contents of their special containers into a huge Mason jar. When Tongue Fu's sister does this, he approaches her and introduces himself.

"Whew," she says. "I've been eating hash brownies all morning. This is quite a heavy trip you've picked to lay on someone so thoroughly stoned as I am."

"Did not our mother ever make mention of me?"

"Yes, once. But she may be the only thing you and I have in common."

"I wish only to make contact. May I hold your child?"

"Sure. Here, Kilo"—she carefully passes the baby—"say hello to your Uncle Tongue."

"I have never held a child before."

A totally non-verbal quarter-of-an-hour later, Tongue Fu leaves, just in time to join that group of disgruntled dairy industry conventioneers, all being given free samples of *Maharishi Hashish Yogurt*.

On his way to store his yogurt stash in the office refrigerator, Tongue Fu spots the frankfurter maker, weeping bitterly into his sauerkraut.

"That fuckin' Department of Agriculture," he cries. "Now they're gonna permit fatty hog jowls to be used in hot dogs. I'm so discouraged."

An eager passerby pulls a tissue out of a box and hands it to the frankfurter maker. "Here, wipe away your tears with this."

The tissue has a stenciled portrait of an obese teenager with the caption: *Who Is Guru Golly Ji?*

The frankfurter maker blows his nose and smears the image.

13

Better Your Exist Strikes Again

In town there's a supermarket with a truck parked in front, filled with cardboard cartons containing foodstuffs. A slide of metal rollers protrudes from the open door on the side of the truck down onto the sidewalk. A separate section of slide protrudes up onto the sidewalk from the basement of the supermarket.

A young black man is standing on the sidewalk between the two sections of slide. A second young black man inside the truck is rolling carton after carton down the slide. The first man catches each carton and puts it on the rollers of the slide going into the basement. He stops periodically to let folks walking on the sidewalk pass through.

You Are the Sunshine of My Life, Stevie Wonder is radio serenading Rosebud Zwalyimeh and Tongue Fu, while she drives the little-American-flag-decal-covered Volkswagen into town, both of them eating *Maharishi Hashish Yogurt* along the way.

She parks the car in the supermarket parking lot, and they walk toward the entrance holding hands.

The slide to the basement gets jammed. The man on the sidewalk starts to adjust the bunched-up cartons, but the man in the truck continues sliding down more cartons. Now the man on the sidewalk must use his other hand in order to keep them back at the same time. "Hold it!" he calls out. "Hold it!"

He's stuck there, with his arms outstretched, inadvertently blocking the only passageway that had remained on the sidewalk.

Rosebud and Tongue Fu arrive at this point. She spontaneously kisses the helpless man on the cheek. Letting go of Tongue Fu's hand, she ducks under the laughing black man's arm....

FLASHICBACKIC:

A black activist, the boyfriend of a younger Rosebud Zwalyimeh, is laughing at her.

"I'm serious," she says. "It gnaws at me to try and identify with *One Man, One Vote.* Even the *I Ching* talks about the superior *man."*

"That's just semantics," he says. "I mean, you know, man *embraces* woman." He attempts to hug her but she pulls away.

"No. I can't separate our personal relationship from the movement. I'm through with double standards. I want equality."

"Do you know that when I was a kid, I wanted to be white so bad that I used a razor blade to make a part in my kinky hair?"

"Well, I worked in a law office and had to bleach the hair on my legs so it wouldn't show through my stockings. So I've been niggerized too."

"We're certainly not the same *emotionally,* though. I could have a casual affair, but it's different with chicks.

You have to get *involved* with every guy you sleep with."

"First of all, I'm not a *chick*. But I just want the option to have the *right*— to get involved with any guy I sleep with. That's the risk of freedom. I'm *not* your slave."

"You mean I'm not supposed to ever get jealous?"

"That's the last politics," she says. "Jealousy is the difference between love and possession."

"But it's always been so good with us in bed."

"That's not enough any more."

"Sheeeit!" He forces himself sexually upon her.

Just before he comes, he says, "I love you."

"Well," she sobs, "you finally made it. You've become white...."

Tongue Fu kisses the laughing black man on the other cheek, ducks under his other arm and rejoins hands with Rosebud. They separate again to help get the cartons straightened out on the slide. Then they head for the supermarket entrance.

"Open, sesame seed," Rosebud gestures, and the automatic glass door obeys her command.

Tongue Fu gives her a ride in a supermarket cart. Rosebud puts a can of frozen orange juice down his back.

They go on the little stationary rides that are there to divert children from mischief. Then they examine with a haughty air the gourmet delicacy rack.

Tongue Fu picks up a package of truffles and asks a passing clerk, "What are these?"

"A dollar-forty-nine."

Rosebud strolls alongside the meat display counter, printing on the respective price cards with a magic marker, *Dead Cows* and *Dead Pigs* and *Dead Chickens*.

Suddenly three gunshots are heard from outside.

Frizzie-haired Innocence from Camp Crap has apparently killed both of those young black men and then herself. In her pocket is found this handwritten suicide note:

> *There is going to be famine in the United States as well as Pakistan.*
>
> *I cannot bear the thought of living with the knowledge that people are actually starving to death.*
>
> *I shall take the lives of two others along with my own.*
>
> *They are integral parts in the chain of food distribution.*
>
> *They are traitors to their blackness.*
>
> *In keeping with the principle of Better Your Exit, I have decided to make an example of them.*

There will be more such examples by other members unless everyone starts fasting.

This is the most effective way to make that demand known.

I apologize for disturbing your afternoon.

—BYE Communication #2

"It doesn't make any sense," says Rosebud. "She was the one who said 'Live your alternative' on *TV Ching.*"

"Perhaps," replies Tongue Fu, "this was her alternative."

14

Guru Golly Ji Gets Taken for a Ride

Surrounded by his official entourage, Guru Golly Ji chomps on French-fried potatoes, licks a frozen strawberry custard and gazes at himself in a distortion mirror at the amusement park that a bunch of Camp Crappers are visiting.

Tongue Fu invites him to go on the roller coaster. "I accept," he says. "I could use a new metaphor. Life is like a roller coaster."

"Do you enjoy—going on the rides here?"

"Listen, they all try to squeeze enjoyment from out of fear. But if somebody ain't afraid, then that's enjoyment also. Outasight."

As their roller coaster car ascends the tracks, Guru Golly Ji folds his arms across his chest. When everyone else screams on the descent, he maintains a peaceful facade, even on the steepest decline.

Nevertheless, he throws up. His divine vomit curves around and lands on the note-pad of Primo Colombian, who is sitting next to Notary Sojak in the seat behind....

❀

FLASHIEBACKIE:

Six-year-old Golly Ji is a pupil at the Famous Gurus School.

"I don't wanna be a famous guru," he wails.

His teacher places an electronic stimulator against Golly Ji's thigh. He reels with pain. "Now behave yourself or you'll get another contingency shock."

"I'm sorry. I'm ready for today's lesson."

"All right. Now then. What is the value of nostalgia in recruiting converts?"

"To associate feelings of warmth with the famous guru."

"What is the value of ritual in recruiting converts?"

"To make security under the famous guru more desirable than change."

"What is the value of sacrifice in recruiting converts?"

"To reinforce dependency on—ah, please, can't I just go out and play with the other kids?"

The teacher gives Golly Ji's other thigh a taste of the electronic stimulator. He reels with pain once again. "Now let's get on with your catechism. The value of sacrifice?"

"To reinforce dependency on the famous guru through the concept of cognitive dissonance...."

On the ground again, Tongue Fu introduces Guru Golly Ji to Wormer Slickheart, the founder of *Spiritual Materialist Training,* better known by its initial letters, SMT.

After a snack of corn-on-the-cob and lime slush, the trio goes on the ferris wheel, where Slickheart addresses himself to Guru Golly Ji as though he were a captive audience.

"I'm weird, you're weird. We both get rich off our followers. But there's a difference. Your followers give up all their material possessions to you. Whereas, mine have the satisfaction of giving me a healthy chunk of their cake *plus* continuing to eat the rest of it themselves.

"By applying the spiritual training received at my seminars—such as aggressive eye contact, for example—to *sales* techniques, why, they can proceed to build up their income at a geometrically increasing rate. Or what's a growth movement *for?*"

That evening in the Camp Crap office, Captain Media-freak and Chocolate Graham are watching *The NBC Nightly News* on a portable black-and-white television set.

David Brinkley is reciting his Journal: "The dichotomy between the theory and practice of harmonious living at Camp Crap in Oregon has been further underscored with the second American Kamikaze action by an individual from there. She has been identified only by the putridly ironic name, Innocence.

"Lacking any rational motivation, she shot and killed two young black men and then took her own life, leaving a suicide note which included a reference to Better Your Exit.

"Originally, that mysterious organization had as its main precept the attack on institutions considered to be evil. But now, apparently, they have escalated their tactics to include the murder of human beings they don't even know personally, and then they have the unmitigated gall to try and convince us that such acts are committed out of hypersensitivity."

"The FBI has entered the case and revealed today that another detached Oriental ear was found inside the truck where the shooting took place. Supposedly the double assassination was a spiritually inspired warning against impending famine. Well, *Isaiah: 58* suggests, 'Share thy bread with the hungry,' but it doesn't say anything about destroying people who merely happen to be delivering food to a supermarket.

"Reporters who ordinarily limit their professional sidetaking to sports and the weather have recently been expressing their dismay publicly about this particular tragedy, but that's understandable because a great many people they've interviewed at Camp Crap seem to be so much into grasping for their own personal salvation that they remain unperturbed by the horror around them.

"Their rationalizations range from 'What can I do about it anyway?' to 'Well, that's just their karma.' One veteran of the psychedelic revolution seemed to sum it up when he complained that someone had stolen his sleeping bag on which he had painted the slogan, *Property Is Theft.* —John?"

"Thank you, David," says John Chancellor. "We'll have news about increased fighting in the Middle East that could easily erupt into World War Three, but first this important message."

An announcer asks: "Are you having difficulty choosing between the mouthwash you *hate* the taste of and the mouthwash you *love* the taste of? Well, now there's a revolutionary new product for the thoughtful consumer—*Yin-Yang Mouthwash...."*

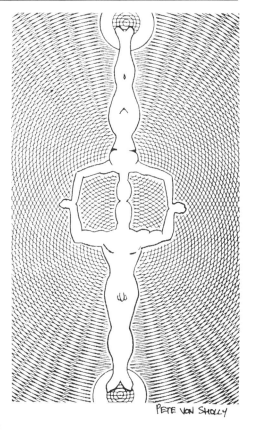

PETE VON SHOLLY

Chocolate Graham and Captain Mediafreak are busy kissing and groping each other, as they do during every commercial.

15

The Contraception Carnival

Balloons emblazoned with Monarch butterflies mating are tied to the trees. Balloons with red and yellow polka dots are being carried around by children. Balloons with sailboats on waves of greenish-blue are skittering above grandparents.

Up close each balloon reveals its false legend: *For the Prevention of Disease Only.* Camp Crap is having a Contraception Carnival.

The musical strains of *Too Many People* boom out over the festivities through the public address system.

"Guess how many birth control pills are in this jar," invites a pre-pubescent barker, "and win a free trip to the overpopulated land of your choice!"

"Take a guided tour through the Fallopian tubes," shouts another. "Learn about our reproductive system from the inside!"

Along the midway, gurus and disciples are playing Miniature Frisbee with surplus diaphragms.

There is a dazzling display of costume jewelry designed entirely out of intrauterine devices and library paste.

An ongoing demonstration of Tantric Yoga keeps turning spectators into volunteers. But a Vasectomies-While-You-Wait stand has no customers at all.

The most popular attraction is *Semenchase,* consisting of several spermatozoa-shaped wheel-carts, which can be propelled forward only by repeated pelvic thrusts of the passengers. The first one to reach the goal—a giant replica of an ovum—is declared "Fertilizer". Bets are taken on the winner of each race, with all proceeds going to the Oregon branch of Planned Parenthood.

"I'm sorry to bother you," Primo Colombian is saying to Tongue Fu, "but did you know that you have absolutely no identity?"

"Our computer check," explains Notary Sojak, "indicates that you have no birth certificate; no alien immigration or naturalization papers; no credit cards or charge plates; no bank accounts; no elementary or high-school diplomas; no university registration; no residence; no telephone or gas and electricity accounts; no validated employment pass or badge; no evidence of treatment at any hospital; no registration with Selective Service; no military discharge; no Veterans Administration number; no Blue Cross or other insurance; no welfare case number; nothing at Internal Revenue; no motor vehicle

operator's license; no arrest record—except for an obscenity bust where the charges were withdrawn—no fingerprints on file; no passport; no Social Security; and not a single membership in any recognized organization,"

"But," says Tongue Fu, "I know—who I am."

"And so do I," adds Rosebud Zwalyimeh, who happens to have a can of Emko Foam in her hand, and with its whipped-cream-like contents she reaches up to decorate the top of Sojak's hairless head with a spermicidal peace symbol. "There. That's because you work for people who have a vested interest in the tools of destruction."

When Colombian and Sojak leave, Rosebud says to Tongue Fu, "Well, the Contraception Carnival seems to be an appropriate environment to tell you. I think I'm pregnant. At least my period is late. But I can't be positive whether you're the father—in which case I'd want to have the baby—or if it's Serpento's, in which case I'd want to get an abortion."

"Yet are we not all one?"

"Oh, sure, but some of us are more one than others...."

FLASHICBACKIC:

"I just fucked a man," Rosebud is telling Chocolate Graham, "who has been personally responsible for torturing and killing hundreds of people on the other side of the world. Serpento. I let him seduce me because I was trying to test him. But I still don't know whether to trust him or not."

"Pretended intimacy has a way of boomeranging," says Chocolate. "You know, I started fucking when I was *five years old*. Pygmies don't have that kind of hangup. After I was kidnapped to America I could see clearly that what keeps this whole *culture* going is the manipulation of your sexual energy."

"But when I told Tongue Fu I'd slept with somebody else, he didn't even mind. Maybe I was testing him too. He's the first man I've gone with who doesn't treat me like private property."

Chocolate clasps Rosebud's hands in her own and muses: "That kind of monogamy would be just another form of kidnapping. just like dating is a form of prostitution. Hookers simply eliminate all the middle-people. The product is sold directly from the factory to the consumer. But, speaking of testing, did you see that anti-evolutionist guy on *TV Ching* the other night, who said that God put fossils on the earth in order to test our faith?..."

❧

"I'm dismayed about the Contraception Carnival," an astrologer is saying on *TV Ching,* "because it's concerned with the quantity of people on our planet, but ignores the quality. Did you know that there is an inescapable correlation between those who are born under the sign of Scorpio and the need to be authoritarian? Now my solution is easy. All we have to do is promote a universal boycott of intercourse-leading-to-conception for, let us say, only six weeks out of every year, from mid-January to the end of February, and within a few generations Scorpios could be completely eliminated from existence without the necessity of resorting to violence."

The astrologer is followed in *TV Ching* by a naturalist who states: "Although I'm not a Catholic, I am opposed to all forms of artificial birth control on the grounds of health and esthetics. But there is a way of determining precisely when you are ovulating by the simple method of taking your own temperature."

The naturalist in turn is followed by a pair of camp jesters wearing fool's caps and harlequin spectacles, who periodically sit on the twin toilets and engage in snappy dialogue.

First Jester: "Say, do you know how they originally discovered what normal temperature is?"

Second Jester: "Why, no, but it certainly must be fascinating."

First Jester: "Well, first they got five hundred people and took all their temperatures."

Second Jester: "What'd they take their temperatures with?"

First Jester: "With five hundred thermometers, silly."

Second Jester: "And then what'd they do?"

First jester: "Well, they added up all the temperatures, and then they took an *average* of all of them from out of the *total.*"

Second Jester: "And—you mean?"

First Jester: "Yes. It was exactly ninety-eight point six."

Second Jester: "Ain't technology wonderful?"

16

The Anal Roberts Revival

Sawdust provides the carpeting inside the mammoth circus tent.

The organist is playing a medley of popular religious songs ranging from *I Believe* to *I Don't Know How to Love Him* to Phil Och's vision of *The Crucifixion.*

Members of the congregation keep looking around, hoping to see others they know sitting in the rows upon rows of wooden folding chairs, all facing a speaker's platform above which are hung crutches, braces and wheelchairs as tangible testimony to past faith healings.

Tongue Fu and Rosebud Zwalyimeh sit thoughtfully munching a mixture of sunflower seeds, raisins and powdered psilocybin.

The master of ceremonies introduces a retired rock'n'roll star who speaks with a static enthusiasm as though he were reading from nonexistent cue cards.

"I once had what I thought was everything. Money. Fame. Power. But something was lacking in my life. I didn't know what. I would travel with my band from city to city. We had our own bus. Our road manager always arranged for us to stay at a Holiday Inn. It was like our home. Everything was always the same. The same interior decoration. The same food. Even the disinfectant they cleaned the rooms with smelled the same. The audiences were the same. The groupies were the same. The drugs were the same.

"And then one day I was bored as usual. I got stoned but that didn't help. Something made me open the drawer and start reading the motel *Bible*. I really got into *The New Testament*, which inspired me to write a hit song. You may remember it: *Saviour Time!*" The crowd applauds and hoots. "But the more I performed it at concerts the more I realized how hypocritical my success was. So I quit show business and joined the Anal Roberts Crusade. And I'd like to sing that hit song for you here at this great revival meeting where it's truly appropriate. I hope you'll clap hands and join in on the chorus."

> *Used t'be depraved, now I'm saved,*
>   *now I'm saved*
>
> *Used t'be enslaved, now with Christ*
>   *my heart is paved....*

Anal Roberts himself—with massive chest, jutting jaw and arcing pompadour—paces around, microphone in fist, resembling a nervous centaur on a leash. Combining the laying on of hands with the power of proper patter, he seems to transfer his vibrant energy to each individual who, one after another, walks, hobbles or is wheeled up a ramp onto the platform from a long line of diseased and crippled hopefuls.

He heals the gout and the goiter. He restores hearing and makes piles disappear. He brings St. Vitus' Dance to a halt and relieves the heartbreak of psoriasis. He cures migraines and eurenesis alike.

Finally Rosebud Zwalyimeh reaches the head of the line. She approaches Anal Roberts.

"Ah, yes, young lady, you look pretty healthy to me. Exactly what is the nature of your affliction?"

"I have an unwanted pregnancy."

"Hmmmm. That's the strangest request I've had since I was once asked to cure an entire lame duck Congress." He chuckles and puts one hand on her abdomen. "Oh, Gawd," he pleads into the microphone, "*heal* this delayed menstruation!" His whole body is trembling uncontrollably. "Yes, Gawd, I feel your strength surging through me now. Heal! *Heal! HEAL! Yeeeeeooooowwwwwwiiiiieeeee!!!* "

Tongue Fu watches with a certain sense of bewilderment....

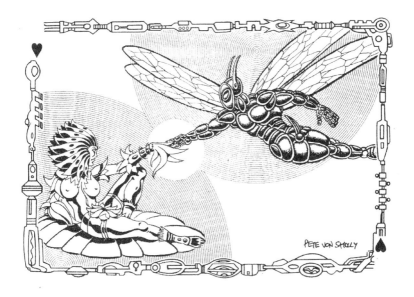

PETE VON SHOLLY

FLASHIEBACKIE:

Post-adolescent Tongue Fu, walking along the beach, automatically stoops to pick up a piece of jagged glass and places it in the pail he now carries for this purpose.

"Put it back in the sand, Anteater," says Luke Warm Sake.

"But, years ago, Say When Daddy taught me to practice such responsibility." His shaved head glistens in the sun. "It is second nature to me now."

"Precisely why you must unlearn that lesson. It is just as much second nature for others to *leave* a piece of glass in the sand. When you learn to experience *their* conditioning by reversing your own, you will begin to make awareless choices."

"But have I not already been making *ethical* choices?"

"To survive, Anteater, you must take nothing for granted. Remember that all of the others believe that their choices are ethical, too. That is *their* means of survival."

They continue walking. Tongue Fu sees the rusty top of a tin can sticking out of the sand. He automatically stoops to pick it up. As he is putting it into his pail, Luke Warm Sake taps him on the arm and quietly waves his forefinger in the air.

"Oops," says Tongue Fu. "I have forgotten with much hurry."

"Try to focus your bellybutton on each instant. That is the reason we tattoo the third eye on a Patoonga priest."

"But tell me, Luke Warm Sake, will I not begin to take my focusing for granted?"

"Then you must focus on your very act of focusing, Anteater."

"And will that give me cosmic perspective?"

"It will get you high...."

"You must be *born* again...." Anal Roberts is delivering his sermon now"... and Jeezus must be your midwife! Jeezus is available for each one of us if we only knew where to look! People nowadays think that the Messiah is going to appear on *The Dating Game!* But I'm here to tell you that the place to look for Jeezus is up your *ass!*"

"Hallelujah!" voices in the congregation respond.

"Yes, I said Jeezus is up your *ass!* And we all *know* that in our secret heart of hearts! I have never met a single human being who didn't stick their finger up their ass when they were alone and then proceed to *smell* their finger! I have only met human beings who won't *admit* they do it!"

"Amen!" voices in the congregation respond.

"But Jeezus stuck *his* finger up *his* ass and smelled it for *all of us!* That is an act of humility! That is an act of acceptance! That is an act of surrender! That is an act of *Jeezus!* When we stick our fingers up our asses and then smell our fingers, we are acting just as *Jeezus* did!"

"Praise the Lord!" voices in the congregation respond.

"I'm going to ask you to come forward now," he says softly, "up here around this platform, walking *with* your *fingers up your asses! Do* you want to feel the compassion of Jeezus? Then I urge you to stick your finger up your ass and smell it! Come on, my dear friends, make that commitment to Jeezus now! Do not be embarrassed to perform this gesture in front of your friends!"

Members of the congregation are streaming down the aisles with fingers up their asses and tears in their eyes.

"That's the way! Nothing to be ashamed of! I feel sorry for those of you who don't have the courage to admit publicly—yes, in front of *strangers*—what you do privately. Let us be open about our humanity! Let's stick those fingers up our asses and smell'em *real good!* Let us decide to identify with Jeezus and change our *lives!* We are all going to smell our fingers *together!"*

Additional converts keep joining the flow, many with such anxiety that it appears they are *pushing* themselves forward with their inserted fingers.

The organist accompanies the retired rock'n'roll star as he bellows with magnificent vibrato the hymn *I Found Jesus in a Dingleberry.*

"Now let's bow our heads. Let us take our fingers out of our asses. Let us smell them and let us feel the joy *of Jeezus* as we do."

A sea of upraised forefingers fills the tent.

Still seated, Tongue Fu reaches underneath, sticks his finger up his ass and smells it. Rosebud, however, sticks *her* finger up her vagina. Then she removes her finger, holds it up and smells the drop of blood on the tip.

Tongue Fu reaches across with his tongue and licks the drop of blood off the tip of her finger. Rosebud smiles as they share this moment of intimacy.

17

Baba Blabla
Breaks His Silence

"At eleven-thirty on *TV Ching* this evening," Chocolate Graham announces over the public address system, "Baba Blabla is going to speak for the first time in thirty years." Then she puts on a record of *New Speedway Boogie* by the Grateful Dead:

> *Please don't dominate the rap, Jack*
> *If you got nothin' to say....*

All day long there is speculation about what Baba Blabla's first words will be.

"Mama," suggests one devotee.

"Where's the dope," guesses another.

Baba Blabla is preceded on *TV Ching* by a man who has disguised his appearance by wearing panty-hose over his face. The legs of the panty-hose are draped around his shoulders like a nylon shawl.

"I'm a spiritual junkie," he confesses. "To support my habit, I travel around to different ashrams and steal all the shoes that have been left outside.

Then I sell them to a fence who supplies a chain of used shoe stores. With the money I earn on each expedition, I'm able to find a new teacher to spend it on so that I can eventually understand how I fit so perfectly into the grand scheme.

"Recently I went and got programmed for forty days at Aripoff Center in Chile where there were some U.S. Army colonels hanging around. Then I went and got *de*programmed for forty nights at Exedrin Institute in Big Sur where I recognized those same colonels hanging around, only now they were generals.

"Well, one night I was soaking in the hot spring sulphur baths and I overheard them discussing a scenario that gave me the chills. They were talking about a squad of their personnel from Special Forces who plan to claim that they're revolutionary BYE terrorists and hold our whole *government* hostage with just a few home-made nuclear devices.

"I didn't want to get involved, but I just had to tell somebody. The information was bursting inside of me. And when I found out that Baba Blabla was holding listening sessions here at Camp Crap, I figured he would be the ideal being to unburden myself to. So I told him this morning, and you could see that he was really startled.

"He wrote out a note saying, *Why don't you expose this?* And then—without the slightest premeditation—I did something I'd never done before. I challenged a guru. I said to him, 'Baba Blabla, I'll expose this on the day you break your silence.' Then he looked even *more* startled. He wrote, *Maybe.* Well, obviously, he later accepted my deal. So without further ado, it gives me great pleasure to introduce him. And now—herrre's *Baba!*"

Wearing a bright orange jalaba, Baba Blabla enters and embraces the spiritual junkie, who quickly pulls up his pants but does not remove the pantyhose from his head as he leaves.

The largest crowd ever to gather on the *TV Ching* field watches Baba Blabla take his place on the toilet. He milks the suspense for a couple of minutes, then opens his mouth and begins to whisper:

"Unaccustomed as I am to public speaking...."

FLASHIEBACKIE:

Little Ricky Blabla, who seems like an ordinary ten-year-old kid, is riding in a car with his parents. Sitting in the back seat, he decides to try out his first dirty joke on them.

"If it takes nine months for a baby to be born, how come you two were in such a hurry when you were making love last night?"

"What?" his mother shrieks, turning to her husband. "Wherever does he pick *up* filth like that?"

"Ricky, I don't want to hear another word out of you," his father threatens through clenched teeth. "Do you hear me?"

No answer. Ricky Blabla is taking his father literally.

"I said I don't wanna hear another word out of you," his father repeats, turning around and raising his right hand as if in the middle of playing four-wall handball. *"Do you hear me?"*

Ricky Blabla remains silent. His father smashes at him with the heel of his hand, but Ricky ducks. His father loses control of the car, it crashes and Ricky becomes an accidental orphan.

Not another word is heard out of him....

"I simply lost the desire to talk," Baba Blabla is explaining on *TV Ching.* "There was nothing physiologically wrong. Relatives had me examined by child psychiatrists who were convinced I was exhibiting—according to their diagnosis—hysteric manifestation of oral necrophilia. Naturally I considered speaking again, but I didn't want to be pressured into it.

"Then I grew *accustomed* to being silent. Matter of fact, I *preferred* it. Most people, in order to look you in the eyes, have to *say* something. That's the *only* time they look you in the eyes. You can't just *stare* at another person. It's considered rude. And I discovered that adults would share the most *bizarre* confidences with me. Through their perception I had become a human pet, who always understood but never judged.

"Then, as I got older, they began to give me *credit* for releasing their inhibitions. My reputation spread. Visitors even came to see me from other countries. And all I had to do was *listen,* as if I were holding auditions for a theater of private pilgrimages.

"Of course I became entrenched in my role because it was a full-time part. I didn't go into the closet when I was alone and make small talk with myself. So there I was, a blossoming intercontinental celebrity, with no idea of what I would have become had fate not cast this gimmick my way.

"I had the advantage of not dissipating energy by trying to select conversation that would imprint me favorably onto the consciousness of others. Conversely, it was a tremendous learning arena. I began to view the world in terms of a psychic chess game between the forces of control and the forces of service. Until today. That spiritual junkie has called my bluff. I had to ask myself, '*Am I stuck in* my *desire to remain silent?*'

"I wandered all around Camp Crap. I watched some fellow with a tongue that's over a foot long playing with children. He used his tongue as a jump-rope for some youngsters. He let others actually *chin* on it. He entertained a group of mothers nursing their infants by getting inside a basket and letting them be snake-charmers, with his tongue as the snake, while one of them played his kazoo.

"Somehow, it was his behavior that made me realize that the *real* contest between control and service is sustained within each *individual.* My silence therefore, was not neutral. Rather, it was aligning me on the side of control. I immediately sought out the spiritual junkie and changed my *Maybe* note to *Yes.* We are what we pretend to be...."

Baba Blabla is followed on *TV Ching* by Virginia Real from the Nude Exorcist Parlor.

"All over the planet," she begins, "people are possessed by their own power. Will there ultimately be a world-wide religious war between those who believe we are all one and those who don't?..."

18

About the Loss of Innocence

The summer of Camp Crap is coming to an end.

Captain Mediafreak wakes up early in the morning. He places his face close to Chocolate Graham's and synchronizes his breathing with hers.

At 7 o'clock, he plugs in the television set. Last night they watched *Tomorrow*. Now he tunes in *Today*. He listens to the sound through a button in his ear so as not to wake up Chocolate.

"In the Better Your Exit case," Barbara Walters is reporting, "the witness who originally saw two men pouring gasoline on that first self-styled Kamikaze motorcyclist has disappeared.... The Dionysius Space Flight could possibly go out of orbit, according to—"

Captain Mediafreak switches from NBC to CBS.

"One of our astute film editors," Hughes Rudd is saying, "remembered seeing the face of Innocence before, and dug up this out-take from The Human Be-In—remember it?—at Golden Gate Park in San Francisco back in Jnuary of 1967."

"I'm a mutation," says the frizzy-haired hippie with a diffraction disc on her forehead. "That's all I know."

White block lettering that reads CHARLOTTE WOMAN-DAUGHTER is superimposed across her chest.

An interviewer's voice asks, "What do you mean, a mutation?"

She answers, "Well, you know, if you were with the Bland Corporation, and you projected into the future all these young dropouts who are going around sniffing flowers instead of fighting with the military or going ape (bleep) over every new kitchen appliance, *you'd* consider us mutations. You'd write a report that said, 'Oh, this is a *bad litter;* we better poison the whole lot of them with strychnine before they spread.'"

The interviewer's voice asks, "How do you feel about fraternizing with the enemy?"

Charlotte grins and says, "Hey, there's a lot of suppressed poets and painters and musicians hiding under straight people. You shouldn't try to divide us. That's propaganda, man."

Captain Mediafreak notices that among the crowd in the background, Notary Sojak is pointing out Innocence to Primo Colombian....

FLASHIEBACKIE:

Captain Mediafreak's mother has come to visit him at the abandoned Times Square newsstand and meet his new roommate, Tongue Fu.

"It will really be wonderful," she is saying, "for the two of you to get away from the city. It's so hot and muggy here in the summer. But won't you miss your television?"

"I'm thinking of taking the set with me on the plane," Captain Mediafreak says. "I'm gonna buy a ticket for it. We'll sit next to each other and fasten our seat-belts when the stewardess tells us to. And she'll serve it a TV Dinner."

His mother is sitting on an old stack of Ed Sanders' mimeographed *Fuck You: A Magazine of the Performing Arts,* sewing name tapes onto everything in sight—clothes, toothpaste tube, motion-picture camera—when she asks Tongue Fu, "Isn't all this media stuff a contradiction of that philosophy of yours about not getting caught in the past?"

"The earth is a living organism. And the media are the nervous system of the earth. If the media are healthy, the earth is healthy. If the media are diseased, the earth is diseased."

"Well, I reckon it's the old question," says Mrs. Mediafreak. "Which came first, the earth or the media?"

"Which came first," Tongue Fu asks in return. "You or your nervous system?"

"Oh, I couldn't answer *that,*" she says. "But you just make sure my little Captain Stumpy here writes to me from camp every day—so I'll know *he's* healthy, I don't care about the earth—just a postcard is all I ask...."

❁

"Let's make a baby today," Rosebud Zwalyimeh says to Tongue Fu.

"We will do it on Coincidence Cliff."

"Where else? My favorite place in all of Camp Crap."

"The child shall choose its own name."

"Okay, but we'll call it "Fun", at least until then. All I've ever really wanted to do was have Fun. And that name could fit either a girl or a boy."

"It could also be either Japanese or American. Fun Fu. The name pleases me."

"No, not Fun Fu. Fun Zwalyimeh."

"Is it not the custom to give a child the name of the father?"

"I've figured that one out. The reason is, you always know who the *mother* is, but sometimes you can't be absolutely positive who the *father is,* so they give a baby the ostensible father's name because it'll imply he's definitely the father."

"I would like—to make a film record—on the development of Fun."

"Captain Mediafteak could film the birth in our home."

"Beyond birth," says Tongue Fu. "I would like to film—us—as we fuck today—for Fun to be able to witness its own conception."

"But we'll use the tripod. And put all the equipment out of the way behind the bushes. And have it prepared in advance. Then we'll take some MDA first." And so they do.

They are kissing as they softly undress each other. Rosebud caresses Tongue Fu's outstretched tongue with her own, first the entire length of the underside, then along the top, spiralling around the matrix of papillae. And then, while she purses her lips over the tip, he begins to withdraw his tongue, slowly, bringing her closer and closer to him.

They seem to melt to the ground. Rosebud is resting on her back, legs apart, knees in the air.

"I will respect your wish," Tongue Fu promises, "and never say—I love you—but I will always be thinking it."

Now he is gently separating the petals of her cunt with the swirls of his tongue, then ever so gradually slithering in deeper and deeper and deeper.

Suddenly Rosebud's body twitches. "You sexist pig," she says. And hits Tongue Fu on top of his head with a rock, knocking him unconscious.

She pulls his tongue out of her. Drags him to the edge of Coincidence Cliff, his head bleeding and his

tongue still drooping from his mouth. She pushes him off the cliff. And then jumps off herself

Over the public address system the Rolling Stones are singing *Wild Horses.* Captain Mediafreak is playing disc jockey.

PETE VON SHOLLY

19

Rosebud's Suicide Note

Tongue Fu regains consciousness.
He makes his way toward Rosebud's broken body. She is
dead.

The poignant sound of Joan Baez singing *Villa
Lobos* is heard across Camp Crap as Tongue Fu
struggles up the steep cliff, carrying Rosebud under
one arm, and grasping foliage for support alternately with his other hand and his tongue.

When he reaches the top, he starts to gather
their clothing and finds a handwritten note in
Rosebud's pocket. Although his vision is blurred, he
manages to read it.

> *Before I take my own life, I'm going to kill
> Tongue Fu, the man who thought he was my
> lover, but who is in reality a symbol of Japa-
> nese imperialism.*
>
> *They take our oil.*
>
> *They take our lumber.*
>
> *They take our whales.*
>
> *And what do they give in return?*

Pollution of the air.

Pollution of the water.

And pollution of the mind.

They flood America with radios, televisions, phonographs.

They take away jobs from our car makers.

Then they sell us cameras to take pictures of the unemployment line.

They are buying up our land.

And they are sneaking in their anti-Christ religion.

You'd think those lousy Japs had won the war the way they're acting.

I'm filled with despair when I see what they are doing to the ecology.

But through the grace of Better Your Exit I'm leaving behind a ray of hope by taking one of them with me.

—BYE Communication #3

P. S. Enclosed please find one mysterious Oriental ear, the BYE's calling card, to help you hear us crystal clear.

Tongue Fu finds the ear in her pocket. He walks to the edge

of Coincidence Cliff, prepares to jump, changes his mind and comes back. He starts to write a note, but stops. Instead, he kneels beside Rosebud, in front of the bush behind which he had placed the motion picture equipment.

"I will speak my suicide note on film. It is difficult—to know where to begin. For I would never have known Rosebud—if I had not known Chocolate Graham. I would never have known Chocolate—if I had not known...."

FLASHIEBACKIE:

At the police station, Tongue Fu hangs up the telephone.

Buff Mogul, the theater manager he was arrested with at *Deep Throat,* is scratching his sideburn with excitement.

Back in their cell, he asks, "Hey was that your real tongue you dialed the number with or just a novelty item?"

"It is my real tongue."

"Do you realize what a fantastic film we could make about you? I can get Sam Peckerpal to direct. My attorney, Albert Morse Code, is coming here to bail us out. I'll have him draw up a contract."

"I am not an actor."

"You wouldn't have to act. just play yourself. That's what we all do anyway. Hey, listen, I don't go around every day offering to back a full-budget flick on the spur of the moment, but you've got a unique box-office attraction there."

"I do not wish to exploit my tongue."

"Lemme see it again, huh?..."

FLASHIEBACKIE
WITHIN FLASHIEBACKIE:

"You must always remember," Say When Daddy is telling young Tongue Fu, "that whether your gift of tongue is to be a curse or a blessing depends on how skillfully you learn to manipulate it. Only after you have thoroughly mastered the art of liberation will you be able to flow with the commerce of exploitation, which is the other side of that coin along whose ridged edge you wish to roll through life. All right, Anteater, you may put your tongue back in your mouth now...."

"That," says Buff Mogul, "is one hellava tongue. You better put it back inside before I flip out. Listen—exploit, *shm*exploit—you'd be able to reach an awful lot of people."

"Perhaps so. But do not call me. I will call you...."

Tongue Fu is still prostrate beside Rosebud's body while Bob Dylan is wailing *It's All Over Now, Baby Blue.* On the line, "Take what you have gathered from coincidence," he hears a buzzing and looks up in the sky. A squadron of jet bombers is flying by in *OM* formation.

Part Three

20

The Parting Advice of Say When Daddy

Into the plush Hollywood office of Buff Mogul Productions walks a secretary carrying a tray with four already-rolled marijuana joints. Tongue Fu, Buff Mogul, Sam Peckerpal and Albert Morse Code each take one, light up and continue their conference.

Buff Mogul: "*You* wanna make a *suicide* film? You mean you would actually kill yourself right on camera? You'd miss opening night and all the reviews and everything."

Albert Morse Code: "There's a legal question to be considered here. It's against the law to commit suicide. That may not make any difference to you, Tongue Fu, but *we* could be charged with being accessories after the fact."

Sam Peckerpal: "Doesn't it depend on how he plans to do it? If he wants to jump off the cliff, we could have a stunt man do that, and then Tongue Fu could commit suicide on his *own* without involving any of us."

Tongue Fu: "You have sworn to me that I would get complete artistic freedom. The film would be a fake—if I do not take my life at the end of it."

Buff Mogul: "Unless you change your mind, right? Listen, you guys, I'm willing to gamble on it. I mean if he has such a strong desire to communicate that he's already postponed his suicide so he can play himself...."

Albert Morse Code: "Oh, there's another thing. Now, Tongue Fu, I know this film is about *your life,* but you're gonna have to compromise on certain scenes. Or are we all prepared to settle for an X rating."

Sam Peckerpal: "Settle? That's what brings *in* the audiences. I have an idea about the female lead, though. I think we should have an *unknown* actress play Rosebud, if only for the sake of image credibility. But we're gonna have one fuckava casting problem for Captain Mediafreak and Chocolate Graham."

Tongue Fu: "No. They have agreed to play themselves." Tongue Fu swivels around in his chair and looks directly into the camera for the first time. "Oonga boonga, Patoonga. Everything you have seen so far is my suicide film. It has been reconstructed from that which I have experienced or observed. Plus what I have learned from conversation with others. The dialogue between Primo Colombian, Notary Sojak and the Chief Coordinator was based on notes that Colombian took at their meeting.

They were written on the inside cover of his notepad, which I picked up at the amusement park in Oregon. Colombian threw his cover away because the divine vomit of Guru Golly Ji had found it."

Tongue Fu takes a toke of his joint, then continues talking to us, smoothly holding back his tears.

"Ah so. Buff Mogul said nine months ago that I might change my mind about committing suicide. I have not. I am unable to stop thinking of Rosebud Zwalyimeh. A Patoonga priest is not supposed to have any attachments. But everything I do aches with the lack of Rosebud. Life itself reminds me of her. Only my own death can do honor to such grief. But there is one more thing I must do first...."

FLASHIEBACKIE:

"I shall no longer call you Anteater," Say When Daddy is telling Tongue Fu. "You are fully matured now."

"Does this mean I am ready for America?"

The blind old man holds out his fist and opens it.

"Quickly, snatch this peyote button—*Zeeeeep*—from my hand." Before Say When Daddy can even finish that sentence, his palm has been emptied by a tongue of almost invisible swiftness. "Time to go, Tongue Fu. Let your hair grow out."

"What shall I do with this peyote button?"

"Take it with you. This is not an ordinary peyote button. It is the essence of *thirteen* peyote buttons, each of sacramental dosage, freeze-dried in our own monastery. You must save this for a time, should it ever come, when you are preparing to take your own life because of failure to uphold Patoonga tradition.

"Not that tradition is all. But as a Patoonga priest you have been trained to maintain a constant balance between tradition and change. Thus, the more you are aware of your personal existence, the more you should simultaneously be aware of your personal nonexistence.

"As a Patoonga priest, you have been taught not to believe in either Heaven or Hell because these places cannot be proven to exist. But this special peyote button will enable you nonetheless to *experience* Heaven or Hell *before* you take your life. I was once ready to commit *hara-kiri*, but my curiosity to taste the journey this sacred button could provide dissolved my compulsion.

"I did not want to give up my option of committing suicide by *committing* suicide. There is no guarantee that you will have the same result. But remember, it is Heaven merely to be able to imagine what Hell would be like...."

"And after I take my peyote button," Tongue Fu is telling us, "I shall end this film. I do not know yet how I will take my life, but—"

The voice of Buff Mogul is heard saying, "Can't you hold off with the peyote till Thursday so you can attend that Beautiful People party tomorrow night?"

The voice of Albert Morse Code says, "Are we gonna film the party too as long as Tongue Fu will be there?"

The voice of Sam Peckerpal says, *"Cut! Cut!* Couldn't you jerks wait with your dumb questions? All right, *take two* on the suicide speech!"

Tongue Fu turns toward them and says, "No. Wait. Let it stay this way."

He turns back facing us and continues: "I do not know yet how I will take my life, but it will not be a way that would disfigure me. I recall that Judy Garland requested a certain makeup artist for her corpse. I would like someone from the circus to give me the face of a clown. Those who pass my casket would then do so with a smile. That would be a way to both better my exit and not hurt anyone.

"But I also do not wish to take up unnecessary space in the earth. So then I could be cremated. And then my family—Captain Mediafreak and Chocolate Graham—could mix my ashes with marijuana and smoke me...."

The voice of Sam Peckerpal says, "Hey, c'mon, Tongue Fu, we could shoot this scene again just for the sake of consistency. Shit, we're not doing *cinema verite* here, y'know."

The voice of Albert Morse Code says, "Yes, we are, for the party scene anyway. Hey, Tongue Fu, you gonna bring a date?..."

21

The Beautiful People Party

Truman Capote is the host of the Beautiful People party at his New York condo, Gossip House.

"Please call me Macho," he tells Tongue Fu with effeminate pride. "All my friends do. I mean you really *have* to be quite macho to go through life just talking like this, don'tcha know?"

Tongue Fu mingles with the other guests. He watches an intense argument, like a tennis game, over whether it is healthier to eat one meal a day or six.

He signs a petition being circulated by Sammy Davis, calling on Ralph Nader to investigate the price of brown rice. He offers a cocktail frankfurter on a yellow toothpick to Helen Gurley Brown, who says, "No, thanks, I'm a vegetarian this month."

"Oh," says Tongue Fu. "Do you eat fish?"

"No, I'm a real vegetarian."

"Well. Do you wear leather?"

"Only my underwear," she replies.

In the kitchen, Tongue Fu joins a group of Hollywood movie stars who are carefully cleaning between their capped teeth with a special roll of dental floss that has been soaked in a cocaine solution.

In the bedroom, he catches someone from Rent-a-Vandal cutting off the sleeves of all the coats and jackets on the bed.

In the bathroom, he listens to Art Linkletter, who is sitting on the sink trying to sell a Plutonium Cluster Bomb Insurance policy to Pat Boone, who is taking an underwater bubble bath with the aid of a snorkel.

Back in the living room, a corporation executive is boasting that he has paid less taxes to support the system than the radical with whom he is debating.

"That'll change," argues the radical, "after the revolution."

"You people want a revolution," replies the executive, "but first you want a good stereo."

"Well, you know what Emma Goldman said—If I can't dance to it, it's not my revolution."

Over in the corner, there is a fervent discussion about the space program.

"I remember the first time a man walked on the moon," Rona Barrett is saying to an astronaut's groupie. "Now, tell me the truth, if you had your druthers, would you rather have seen that escapade on closed circuit television or what really happened at Chappaquiddick on the same night?"

"It doesn't matter either way," answers a practicing Satanist as his pocket is being picked by Billy Graham, "because when the earthquakes and the floods and the pestilence and the plagues of terminal gonorrhea spread around this planet—"

Tongue Fu has to interrupt: "Excuse me. You seem to be—gleeful—about these tragedies."

"Of course I am. Impending devastation is the only thing that gives me any optimism about the future. Would you care for a Quaalude?..."

FLASHIEBACKIE:

"There has always been decadence," the proprietor of a novelty items store is saying. "The Industrial Revolution was just a missing link between the Roman Empire and this portable electric artificial vagina."

Captain Mediafreak is filming this sales pitch to a customer, played by Tongue Fu.

"I wouldn't use it myself—I'm a happily married man but we still live in a democracy. These products were originally intended to collect semen from bulls for the artificial insemination of cows, but they're perfectly safe for humans. However, their use is not recommended if you are a victim of premature ejaculation." "How would I use this artificial vagina?" Tongue Fu asks.

"You plug it in your AC wall socket. Simple enough. This model has a temperature control mechanism which approximates natural vaginal warmth. You can increase the temperature all the way up to Unbearable.

You must lubricate the instrument for maximum efficiency and pleasure. We recommend our own special lubricant which is formulated for optimum viscosity.

You may choose to partially pressurize the instrument before penetration. It has a wide range of adjustability, from a diameter of two inches to entirely closed. This dial here regulates the tiny waves of stimulation which set up a pulsation pattern that aids in ultimately triggering the ejaculatory nerves. Incidentally, we also have a model which plugs right into the cigarette lighter of your favorite automobile. Sometimes you feel like a spot of onanistic pleasure while waiting on line for gasoline. Or even in traffic. On the way home from work seems to be a very popular time."

"How does the deluxe model differ?" Tongue Fu asks.

"The deluxe artificial vagina has rubber folds which, upon inflation, roughly simulate the labia majora and the labia minora just as these tissues are when swollen in actual sexual passion. It also features a three-speed bulbocavernosus muscle which contracts rhythmically. Moreover, it is covered by a soft fabric with skin-like texture—flesh colored—you have your choice of Caucasian, Negroid or Asian. You would probably prefer the Asian. Incidentally, sir, our deluxe model has a special sphincter attachment. Do you happen to suffer from flaccid penis? Of course, this is an optional feature...."

PETE VON SHOLLY

Under the combined influence of cocaine and Quaalude, Tongue Fu leaves the Beautiful People party and goes home to the abandoned newsstand and his artificial vagina.

"You are still a virgin," he says to it, "but not after tonight." First, however, he takes the artificial vagina out to dinner and a movie.

Carrying it in an unmarked storage container, he gets on a bus going to Greenwich Village, where he walks along West 8th Street. He shares an Orange Julius openly with his artificial vagina; doesn't care who sees them together.

On the sidewalk again, he is so zonked out that he bumps into a passerby. "Excuse me," says Tongue Fu, "but do you happen to know when Safe-Driving Day is?"

He continues weaving down the block, stopping at a movie theater where a pornographic martial arts film, *Billy Jackoff,* is playing.

"Two, please," he says to the ticket seller, holding up three fingers.

In the middle of the movie he gets sick and goes to the Men's Room. While retching, he notices that someone has written among the graffiti on the wall of his stall:

ROCKY EATS AFTERBIRTH!

Tongue Fu takes the pen which is attached by a chain to the toilet-tissue dispenser, and he scrawls underneath:

Placenta is good for you!

"There," he says to the artificial vagina, "that will give Rocky food for thought."

And he takes a bus back home. Outside the abandoned Times Square newsstand, an assemblage of youthful zealots sing what sounds to his stoned ears like an obscene chant, perhaps the plaint of an impotent Hindu fakir's wife:

> *Hurry, Krishna! Hurry, Krishna! Krishna, Krishna!*
>
> *Hurry, hurry! Hurry, ram it! Hurry, ram it!*
>
> *Ram it, ram it! Hurry, hurry!*

In his sleeping bag that night, Tongue Fu makes sure that his artificial vagina reaches several climaxes. He passes out before reaching one himself. Later, a burning sensation around his penis wakes him up, but he pulls out the plug of his artificial vagina and goes back to sleep, mumbling: "Rosebud, you belong in the *Ladies' Room....*"

22

Tongue Fu Meets God

With Chocolate at my mother's, says a note on Captain Mediafreak's mini-mattress. *Have a good trip.*

Unscrewing the Oriental head of the jack-in-the-box in his *I Ching,* Tongue Fu removes the Patoonga peyote button he once snatched from the hand of Say When Daddy.

He lets is dissolve in his mouth while he sits prayerfully still. Then he puts an album, *Monterey Hit List,* on the stereo and listens to Otis Redding do *I've Been Lovin' You Too Long;* Janis Joplin do *Bobby McGee;* Jimi Hendrix do *The Star Spangled Banner.*

Tongue Fu sings along with the national anthem—but with lyrics from the previous song—so that instead of "Oh say can you see, by the dawn's early light," he sings "Freedom's just another worrrd … fo-or nothin' left to lose.…"

He turns on the television, channel selector in hand.

Click!

A ventriloquist is performing without a dummy by talking out of sync.

Click!

"Rediscover old values with the Waltons," an announcer is saying, "brought to you by the makers of Wonder Bread and Hamburger Helper. Tonight, John-boy thinks he may be a clairvoyant when he has a dream about a nuclear power plant being constructed on the farm—"

Click!

"We've finally established contact with the team of astronauts further on their way out of orbit," a newscaster is saying as she taps her foot in rhythm with her speech. "Hello, can you hear me up there?... How does it feel knowing that you'll never set foot on earth again?"

Click!

"One nation under Me," a drag queen wearing bright green lipstick and rouge with matching fright wig, is saying, "with barbiturates and amphetamines for all."

She sits at a dressing table playing *Monopoly* with her mirror image, from which she now turns away.

"Oh, there you are, Tongue Fu, I've been waiting for you."

"Who are you?"

PETE VON SHOLLY

"I'm *God,* you silly asshole." Insinuating the voice of Don Rickles.

"Have we not met before? You look—familiar."

"Sure, and I breed contempt. Listen, you dumb freak, you've gotta stop feeling so fuckin' sorry for yourself. I mean it was okay for you to get stoned and watch the news and be really high when the body count came on with *thousands* of war dead every Thursday—oh, where the devil is my Alice Cooper album?—but now you're so selfish as to make such a big deal out of one single person you happened to meet. And you've never even *looked* at that last film of her, that's how much you care."

"It would be too painful."

"Look, dummy, you wanna experience Heaven or Hell while you're still alive, correct-o? Well, the cocksuckin' *truth* transcends Heaven and Hell *both.* I mean I can tell you something that'll just blow your *mind.* There's an interview coming up that Cronkite will do with William 0. Douglas, the Supreme Court Justice, y'know, and he's gonna tell how Franklin D. Roosevelt wanted *him* for Vice-President, with good ol' Harry Truman as *second* choice, only some political hack in Missouri *reversed* the names on the list 'cause Harry was a local boy, and now Douglas is gonna say that if *he* had become President when Roosevelt died, he *wouldn't've* dropped the atomic bombs on Japan. How's *that* grab ya?"

"But if you are God, why would you permit such a thing to happen?"

"That's easy, sonny. Because I'm a fuckin' racist...."

❦

FLASHIEBACKIE:

"I'm not a racist," a man on *TV Ching* is saying. He is Doctor Shocktreat, winner of the Ignobel Prize together with four other scientists for inventing the disposable contact lens. If he were to put on bright green lipstick and rouge with matching fright wig, he could play God perfectly.

"I merely contend as a genetic premise," he continues, "that non-Aryans are *born* with less consciousness than Aryans. Oh, yes, I know how controversial it is to insist that consciousness is hereditary, but unless we're willing to lose the human race, compulsory sterilization is the final solution to the consciousness problem.

"With so many gurus here at Camp Crap who are of other than Aryan background, I can only say that despite their outward manifestation of higher consciousness, they have consistently achieved lower scores on the CQ tests we've devised...."

Tongue Fu has shut off the television and set up the motion picture projector.

Rosebud Zwalyimeh and Tongue Fu are kissing and undressing each other on Coincidence Cliff. "I will respect your wish," he promises, "and never say—I love you—but I will always be thinking it."

Now he is performing cunnilingus upon her. Tiptoeing up from behind him is Serpento. Rosebud sees Serpento and her body twitches. "You sexist pig," she says.

Serpento hits Tongue Fu on top of his head with a rock. Then he does the same to Rosebud.

He pulls Tongue Fu's tongue out of Rosebud's body, drags them one at a time to the edge of the cliff and pushes them off.

Then, not wishing to waste his erection he mastur-
bates hurriedly. Primo Colombian and Notary Sojak
arrive. Sojak says to Serpento, "Gimme an ear."

Serpento takes an ear from his pocket and gives
it to Sojak, who puts it together with a handwritten
note into the pocket of Rosebud's jeans.

Sojak hands Serpento a thick envelope.

"It's not easy pretending to be an honest cop,"
Serpento complains. "I gotta take a lot of shit from
my brother officers."

"Y'know," muses Colombian, "that doesn't square
with what Baba Blabla said about how we are what
we pretend to be."

"C'mon, let's get outa here," Sojak says. "Geez,
that Joan Baez sure sings pretty."

The three leave. Then there is nothing on the
screen for a while except Coincidence Cliff itself.

The film runs out just as Tongue Fu reaches the
top of the cliff with Rosebud under his arm.

Tongue Fu now shuts off the projector and puts
the television back on. The channel he was talking
to God on is blank.

Click!

Tongue Fu is walking with his tongue in Rosebud Zwalyimeh's ear at Camp Crap. Suddenly he
whips his tongue out of her ear and straight ahead;
there is a blurred panning of the landscape.

"That camera-shy young man," the newscaster is
saying, "was Tongue Fu, who is no longer camera-
shy. For the past several months he has been making a feature-length film about his life and tongue.
The son of a Japanese Kamikaze pilot, rumor has it
that Tongue Fu plans to commit suicide at the end
of his film as a publicity stunt—"

Click!

That pair of camp jesters, co-opted from *TV Ch-ing,* now sit on the network's own twin toilets.

First Jester: "Is there ever a spiritual basis for conspicuous consumption?"

Second Jester: "Yes, when an orthodox Jew owns two sets of false teeth, one for meat and one for dairy."

Click!

Tongue Fu is walking west along 42nd Street, carrying Captain Mediafreak in his basket with one hand, and holding Chocolate Graham's hand with the other. She is barefoot.

They pass a drag queen wearing bright green lipstick and rouge with matching fright wig, standing in the doorway of an Adult Bookstore.

Tongue Fu stares at her for a moment, then says: "Thank you, God."

The drag queen stares back at him for a moment, then replies: "God never says you're welcome."

Chocolate Graham slips one of her calling cards inside the drag queen's bright green tote bag.

And Captain Mediafreak scrawls on the wall from his basket: *Rosebud Lives!*

Then the trio continues on, walking into the smoggy sunset.

Click!

Glossary

By David Jay Brown

Adam's Rib: A 1949 film—considered a classic romantic comedy—staring Spencer Tracy and Katharine Hepburn, about a prosecutor who is assigned a case against a woman who tried to scare her adulterous husband by repeatedly shooting him.

Alice Cooper: A popular rock singer and songwriter—with a dark and dramatic edge—who combined heavy metal, garage rock, horror movies, and vaudeville to create a uniquely theatrical style of rock music performance.

Anal Roberts: A parody of Oral Roberts, a Christian televangelist and traveling faith healer. Roberts conducted hundreds of evangelistic and faith healing crusades around the world. He was known for putting his hands on a disabled follower, and yelling very loudly, "Heal! Heal!" During his TV sermons he instructed his viewers to place their hands on the TV screen, while he yelled, "Heal! Heal!", which was suppose to deliver God's divine energy into the ailing viewers to heal them.

Andy Warhol: A painter, avant-garde film maker, record producer, author, and often-quoted celebrity, who became one of the central figures in the Pop Art movement. Warhol was well-known for the unusually diverse social circles that he frequented, and for painting a famous portrait of a Campbells soup can. He died in 1987.

Aretha Franklin: Popular singer, songwriter, and pianist—known largely for soul recording. Franklin is generally considered to be one of the greatest vocalists of all time.

Art Linkletter: The host of the popular, long-running television show, *House Party*—which aired on CBS from 1952 to 1969. Linkletter became famous for interviewing children during a segment of the show called Kids Say the Darndest Things. It was thought that his daughter committed suicide on LSD by jumping out of a window. (See LSD.) Years later Linkletter recanted the story when suspicion was cast upon the boyfriend, who was tripping with his daughter and who was implicated in another girlfriend dying in a fall when he was present.

Baba Blabla: A parody of Eastern philosophy gurus in general. "Baba" is a term of affection for a saint or a holy man that means "father."

Billy Graham: A famous Christian evangelist, who has preached in person to more people around the world than anyone else in human history. Graham has served as a "spiritual adviser" to numerous U.S. presidents.

Black Panthers: A political organization—founded in order to promote civil rights and self-defense for African Americans—that was active within the U.S. during the late 1960s and early 1970s.

Bob Newhart: The star of a television situation comedy, The Bob Newhart Show—that aired on CBS from 1972 to 1978—about a psychologist's dealings with his neurotic patients and fellow office workers.

Carol Burnett: The star of a sketch comedy television show, The Carol Burnett Show—that aired on CBS from 1967 to 1978. The cast members of the show, which included Tim Conway, Harvey Korman, Vicki Lawrence, and Lyle Waggoner, did wacky comedy routines and parodies that were popular during the late 1960s and 1970s.

Chappaquiddick: A small island, part of Edgartown, Massachusetts, where Senator Ted Kennedy attended a party in 1969. After the party, Kennedy drove his mother's car off of a bridge and into a channel, where a young female campaign worker who was in the car with him drowned. Kennedy was accused to doing nothing to save the girl and did not report the accident to authorities until the next morning. entered a plea of guilty to a charge of leaving the scene of an accident, and he received a suspended sentence of two months in jail.

Come on, Baby, Light My Fire: A line from the popular song *Light My Fire*, that was originally performed by the rock band The Doors in 1967.

David Brinkley: A popular television newscaster, who co-anchored NBC's nightly news program, *The Huntley–Brinkley Report*, from 1956 to 1970. Brinkley co-anchored *The NBC Nightly News* for the next thirty years. He died in 2003.

Deep Throat: A pornographic film, released in 1972, about a woman, played by porn star Linda Lovelace, who discovers that her clitoris is mysteriously located in the back of her throat, and that she has to perform oral sex on well-endowed men in order to climax. This X-rated film was widely shown in mainstream movie theaters and condemned by many.

Dick Cavett: An Emmy Award-winning television talk show host—known for his witty intellectual style and in-depth discussion of issues—who, from 1969 to 1996 was the host of his own talk show. Cavett's talk show—The Dick Cavett Show—changed formats and appeared on different television and radio networks over the years.

Emma Goldman: A Lithuanian-born anarchist and feminist. Goldman's writings and speeches played a pivotal role in the development of anarchist political philosophy in the United States and Europe during the first half of the twentieth century. She died in 1940.

Eva Gabor: A Hungarian-born actress, best known as the wife of Eddie Albert's character on the popular television situation comedy Green Acres. (See Green Acres.) Gabor died in 1995.

Freemasons: Members of fraternal organization known as Freemasonry based upon certain shared metaphysical and moral ideals. Freemasonry has existed since at least the mid-1600s, although many people believe that it is actually a lot older. Much about their origins and rituals are shrouded in mystery and secrecy.

Green Acres: A popular television situation comedy—that aired on CBS from 1965 to 1971—starring Eddie Albert and Eva Gabor, about an accomplished attorney living his lifelong dream to be a farmer, and his metropolis-loving wife who is unwillingly dragged along, away from the privileged and glamorous life in New York City that she adored.

Harry Reasoner: A journalist and news commentator, who, in 1968, teamed up with Mike Wallace to start the investigative newsmagazine television series *60 Minutes*, that airs on CBS to this day. Reasoner was the anchorman for *ABC's Evening News* from 1970 to 1978, and then returned to CBS, where he remained, until he retired and died in 1991.

Helen Gurley Brown: Author, publisher, and businesswoman, Brown was the editor-in-chief of *Cosmopolitan* magazine from 1965 to 1997.

He Ain't Heavy, He's My Brother: A 1969 song by The Hollies. The title for the song came from the motto for Boys

Town, a community formed in 1917 by a Catholic priest named Father Edward Flanagan, where troubled or homeless boys could find help.

I Believe: A popular gospel song written in 1953 by Ervin Drake, Irvin Graham, Jimmy Shirl and Al Stillman.

I Ching: An ancient Chinese book of divination and philosophy that is designed to identify order in what seem like chance events. The roots of the *I Ching* can be traced back to the 8th century B.C.

I Don't Know How to Love Him: A song from the Broadway musical and film Jesus Christ Superstar, that was sung by the character of Mary Magdalene. This popular song was written by Andrew Lloyd Webber and Tim Rice.

Jacqueline Kennedy Onassis: The wife of president John F. Kennedy from 1953 to 1963, and of Aristotle Onassis from 1968 to 1975. She had a successful career as a book editor and died in 1994.

Janis Joplin: A singer and songwriter, popular in the Sixties, who became famous as the lead singer of the rock band Big Brother and the Holding Company. Joplin later had a solo career and died in 1970 from a drug overdose.

Jimi Hendrix: Guitarist, singer, and songwriter, who became famous during the Sixties. Hendrix is generally considered to be one of the greatest and most influential guitarists in rock music history. He headlined the 1969 Woodstock Festival and died in 1970 of a drug overdose.

Joan Baez: A folk singer and songwriter, best known for her 1970s hit *The Night They Drove Old Dixie Down*. Baez performed at the 1969 Woodstock Festival. Many of her songs are topical and deal with important social issues.

Johnny Carson: The iconic, witty and charming host of NBC's *The Tonight Show* from 1962 to 1992. Watching Johnny Carson do his opening monologue became a ritual for how millions of people ended their day. Carson died in 2005.

Judy Garland: A film actress and singer, best known for playing the role of Dorothy in the 1939 film *The Wizard of Oz*. She died in 1969.

Linda Lovelace: The star of the pornographic film *Deep Throat*. (See Deep Throat.)

LSD (lysergic acid diethylamide): A powerful psychedelic drug that was widely used by the youth counterculture during the Sixties. LSD experiences played an important role in the development of the counterculture's philosophy, politics, music, and art.

Mary Tyler Moore: The star of a television situation comedy—that aired on CBS from 1970 to 1977—about an independent career woman who works in a television news studio. The show broke new ground, as Moore played a single woman in her thirties who was not widowed, divorced, or seeking a man to support her.

M*A*S*H*: A television situation comedy—that aired on CBS from 1972 to 1983—about a team of doctors and support staff working in a Mobile Army Surgical Hospital during the Korean War. Based upon an earlier novel and film, M*A*S*H* was a dark comedy that presented a realistic look at the atrocities of war.

McMillan and Wife: A crime drama television series—that aired on NBC from 1971 to 1977—about a middle-aged San Francisco Police Commissioner, and his pretty and much younger wife, solving robberies and murder mysteries.

Merv Griffin: A popular talk show host, singer, game show host, and a highly accomplished entertainment entrepreneur, who created the long-running and hugely successful game shows *Jeopardy!* and *Wheel of Fortune.* Griffin is best known for hosting a syndicated television talk show, *The Merv Griffin Show*—that aired across America from 1965 to 1986. He died in 2007.

Moonies: A derogatory term for members of Sun Myung Moon's religious organization, the Unification Movement, which actively targeted troubled or lonely young men for induction into the church. The organization is best known for arranging the largest mass-weddings in history.

No, No, Nanette: A musical comedy—based on a book of the same title by Otto Harbach and Frank Mandel—that was first produced in 1925, about a wealthy Bible publisher and his frugal wife trying to teach their ward, Nanette, to be a respectable young lady.

Norman Mailer: Novelist, journalist, playwright, screenwriter, and film director. Mailer has been awarded the Pulitzer Prize twice and the National Book Award once. He is considered to be an innovator in a genre called "New Journalism," and he was one of the founders of *The Village Voice* in 1955.

Otis Redding: An influential soul singer, probably best known for his delivery of the hit single *Sittin' on the Dock* of the Bay. Redding died in 1967, three days prior to the release of the song that made him the most famous.

Pat Boone: An actor, television host, and singer—with a clean-cut image—who achieved popularity during the 1950s doing cover versions of rhythm and blues songs, although he later performed gospel and country music. Boone is a devout born-again Christian and a conservative political commentator.

Phil Donahue: A media personality and talk show host, best know as the creator and star of the syndicated talk show, *The Phil Donahue Show*, which aired across America from 1970 to 1996. The Phil Donahue Show was the first television tabloid talk show, and it generally focused on controversial political issues that divide liberals and conservatives.

Philip Morris: A 19th Century British tobacco dealer, who created the world's largest commercial tobacco company, which is now a subsidiary of Altria Group, Inc. TV ads featured a small man dressed in a bellhop's uniform who called loudly through cupped hand, "Call for Philip Mooorriiisss".

Phil Ochs: A singer, songwriter, musician, and political activist, known for his humor, humanism, and haunting voice. Ochs performed at many antiwar and civil rights rallies during the Sixties. He died in 1976.

Quaalude: A sedative drug (methaqualone), available by prescription from 1965 to 1984, that became popular as a recreational drug. In 1984 Methaqualone became a Schedule I drug in the U.S. Controlled Substances Act, considered to be the most dangerous of drugs and without any medical use—placing "ludes" in the same category as cannabis, LSD, and heroin. Ludes were a sex enhancer because they quell thoughts and height hen sensual feelings.

Ralph Nader: an attorney and political activist in the area of consumer rights, environmentalism, humanitarianism, and democracy, known for his investigations called "Nader-Raders". Nader has been an outspoken critic of corporate power and he helped to found numerous consumer-protection based organizations.

Rolling Stones: A British rock band, formed in 1962, that is largely led by the song-writing partnership of singer Mick Jagger and guitarist Keith Richards. The Rolling Stones are one of the most commercially successful and critically acclaimed rock bands of all time.

Rona Barrett: A gossip columnist and media personality, who appeared regularly on television during the mid-1960s and 1970s, strongly criticizing well-known Hollywood personalities. Barrett retired in 1991.

Rosicrucians: Members of an esoteric organization, with origins that stretch back, at least, into the 1600s—although many people believe that the order is actually more ancient. The Rosicrucian order is based upon the metaphysical notion that mystical wisdom lies within each individual and that a community of invisible masters is available to assist in humanity's spiritual development.

Sammy Davis Jr.: A popular singer, dancer, actor, standup comedian, and multitalented musician, who helped to breakdown racial barriers in Hollywood. Davis once described himself as "a short, ugly, one-eyed, black Jew" to someone complaining about discrimination. He was often billed as "the greatest living entertainer in the world." He died in 1990.

Scientologeek: A parody of "Scientologist," a member of the Church of Scientology—a philosophical and religious organization, created in 1952 based upon the writings of science fiction and self-help author L. Ron Hubbard.

Slow Death: A counterculture or "underground" comic book that was modeled after the E.C. horror comics of the Fifties, such as *Tales from the Crypt*. (See: Zap.)

Smoke Gets in Your Eyes: A song written for the 1933 Broadway musical Roberta by Jerome Kern and Otto Harbach.

Stevie Wonder: A popular singer, songwriter, and musician, who recorded more than thirty top ten hits in his career. Blind from infancy, he signed on with Motown Records at the age of twelve. Wonder plays numerous musical instruments but is best known for his skills on the keyboard.

That Old Black Magic: A popular song by Harold Arlen and Johnny Mercer, first recorded in 1942. The song has been done by many well-known vocalists, such as Frank Sinatra and Sammy Davis Jr.

The Beatles: A British rock group, largely led by the song-
writing partnership of John Lennon and Paul McCartney,
that became one of the most commercially successful and
critically acclaimed bands in the history of popular music.
John Lennon was assassinated in 1980 and George Harrison died in 2001.

The Bunkers: A family that was portrayed in a popular television situation comedy called *All in the Family,* that ran on
CBS from 1971 to 1979. The "Bunkers" were Archie, Edith,
their daughter Gloria, and her husband Michael. The show
broke new cultural ground in its depiction of issues that
were previously deemed unsuitable for a U.S. network television comedy.

The Dating Game: A television show that ran on ABC from
1965 to 1973, in which a young attractive woman—known
as a "bachelorette"—would question three bachelors, who
were hidden from her view. Occasionally the sex-roles were
reversed. The questioning bachelorette—or bachelor—had
to choose one of the three unseen bachelors—or bachelor-
ettes—for a weekend date in some romantic location.

The Grateful Dead: A rock band, known for its eclectic mix of
improvisational musical styles and live shows, that formed in
San Francisco in 1965 and toured extensively for thirty years.
The lead guitarist for the band, Jerry Garcia, died in 1995.

The Waltons: A television series about a large rural family—seven children, parents and grandparents—that aired
on CBS from 1972 to 1981. The show is seen through the
eyes of the eldest son—John-Boy—and it portrayed their
struggle to make a decent living during the Great Depression and World War II.

Tongue Fu: The name is a parody of a popular television
show, *Kung Fu*, starring David Carradine that ran on ABC
from 1972 to 1975, about a wise Chinese martial arts
master and monk, who wanders around the old American
West reforming bullies. He often gave sage advice to his
grandson who he called, "Grasshopper".

Truman Capote: A popular writer whose novels, plays, stories, and nonfiction books are generally recognized as liter-
ary classics. Capote is the author of *Breakfast at Tiffany's*
and In *Cold Blood*. He died in 1984.

Van Morrison: An Irish singer, songwriter, and musician who is widely considered to be one of the most influential vocalists in the history of rock and roll. Morrison plays a variety of musical instruments, and much of his music has been influenced by soul, R&B, jazz, and Celtic traditions.

W.C. Fields: An actor and comedian who became well-known for creating one of the classic comic personas of the first half of the 20th Century. Fields died in 1946.

Walter Cronkite: A broadcast journalist who was the anchorman for *The CBS Evening News* from 1962–1981. Cronkite was often cited in viewer opinion polls during the 1970s and 1980s as "the most trusted man in America."

William O. Douglas: A U.S. Supreme Court Justice, whose term lasted over thirty-six years, making him the longest-serving justice in the Supreme Court's history. Douglas was known for advocating individual rights. He died in 1980.

Zap: The best-known of the countercultural comic books—known as "underground comix"—that emerged out of San Francisco in the late 1960s. *Zap* was started in San Francisco in 1968, with the work of satirical artist Robert Crumb.

Paul Krassner calls himself an investigative satirist. After *Life Magazine* published a favorable profile of him, the FBI supposedly sent a poison-pen letter to the editor, complaining: "To classify Krassner as a social rebel is far too cute. He's a nut, a raving, unconfined nut."

Krassner published *The Realist* magazine from 1958 to 1974, then reincarnated it as a newsletter from 1985 to 2001. "The taboos may have changed," he wrote, "but irreverence is still our only sacred cow." He demanded a paternity test when *People Magazine* labeled him "Father of the underground press". Krassner is the only person in the world ever to win awards from both Playboy (for satire) and the Feminist Party Media Workshop (for journalism).

Krassner edited Lenny Bruce's autobiography, *How to Talk Dirty and Influence People*, and became a stand-up comic himself, opening at the Village Gate in 1961, but now rarely works the comedy-club circuit, preferring campuses, theaters and art galleries—venues have ranged from a New Age Expo to the Skeptics Conference, from a Neo-Pagan Festival to the L.A. County Bar Association, from a Swingers Convention to the Brentwood Bakery.

In 2004, Krassner received an ACLU Uppie (Upton Sinclair) Award for dedication to freedom of expression. And at the 14th annual Cannabis Cup in Amsterdam, he was inducted into the Counterculture Hall of Fame, which he claimed was his ambition since he was three years old.

PaulKrassner.com

Trina Robbins is a Herstorian, writer and retired cartoonist. She has been writing graphic novels, comics and books for over thirty years. Her subjects have ranged from Wonder Woman and the Powerpuff Girls to her own teenage superheroine, GoGirl!, and from women cartoonists and superheroines to women who kill. Trina has written over a dozen educational graphic novels for three different publishers, provided English language rewrites for shojo manga graphic novels. Trina lectures on comics and graphic novels throughout the United States and Europe. She lives in San Francisco, in a moldering 102 year old house with her cats, shoes, and books.

Books authored by Trina include: *Tender Murders: Women Who Kill, Go Girl: The Time Team, Wild Irish Roses, From Girls to Grrils: A History of Women in Comics, Califa, Queen of California, Nell Brinkley & the New Women of the 20th Century. Eternally Bad: Goddesses with Attitude.* and *Cats Walk.*

Visit Trina's site at:

trinarobbins.com,
mswuff@juno.com.

Pete Von Sholl

Pete is known from one end of his house to the other as a "Hollywood Storyboard Legend" having storyboarded well over 100 feature films—including *The Shawshank Redemption, Darkman, Mars Attacks,* and *The Mist*—but his true passions have always been comics and something akin to pop vandalism! He brought "fumetti" into the digital age with his unique *Morbid and Extremely Weird Stories* graphic novels from Dark Horse. Satire is alive and well with his *Crazy Hip Groovy Go-Go Way Out Monsters* and *Comic Book Nerd* magazines from TwoMorrows. Pete has created 60 cover paintings for *Turok Son of Stone* "comics that never were", a whole new issue of John Stanley's Melvin Monster and a ton of faux Classics *not* Illustrated covers and monster model boxes with Lovecraftian themes just out of love for the subjects. Pete has done a ton of dinosaur illustrations and has three self-published books, which are now sold out— sold out of cartoons cluttering up his house, that is. He has finally become unable to completely ignore the horrible world of politics and the state of our nation and planet, so has teamed with hoary veteran and fellow old hippie underground cartoonist, Denis Kitchen to bring all his skills to bear in a book of monstrous postcards called *Captiol Hell.* Pete is based in Sunland, California. Visit his site at www.vonshollywood.com

David Jay Brown

David holds a master's degree in psychobiology from New York University. He is the author of four bestselling volumes of interviews with leading-edge thinkers, *Mavericks of the Mind, Voices from the Edge, Conversations on the Edge of the Apocalypse,* and *Mavericks of Medicine.* He is also the author of two science fiction novels, *Brainchild* and *Virus.* David did the California-based research for two of British biologist Rupert Sheldrake's books on unexplained phenomena in science: *Dogs That Know When Their Owners Are Coming Home* and *The Sense of Being Stared At.*

David is based in Ben Lomond, California. To find out more about David's work visit his award-winning web site at www.mavericksofthemind.com.